MAD

CW00953342

It was only a m .... before a clever publisher realized that there is an audience for whom *Exile on Main Street* or *Electric Ladyland* are as significant and worthy of study as *The Catcher in the Rye* or *Middlemarch*. . . . The series . . . is freewheeling and eclectic, ranging from minute rock-geek analysis to idiosyncratic personal celebration—*The New York Times Book Review*

Ideal for the rock geek who thinks liner notes just aren't enough—*Rolling Stone*

One of the coolest publishing imprints on the planet—*Bookslut*

These are for the insane collectors out there who appreciate fantastic design, well-executed thinking, and things that make your house look cool. Each volume in this series takes a seminal album and breaks it down in startling minutiae. We love these. We are huge nerds—*Vice*

A brilliant series . . . each one a work of real love—*NME* (UK)

Passionate, obsessive, and smart—*Nylon*

Religious tracts for the rock 'n' roll faithful—*Boldtype*

[A] consistently excellent series—*Uncut* (UK)

We . . . aren't naive enough to think that we're your only source for reading about music (but if we had our way . . . watch out). For those of you who really like to know everything there is to know about an album, you'd do well to check out Continuum's "33 1/3" series of books.—*Pitchfork*

For reviews of individual titles in the series, please visit our website at www.continuumbooks.com and 33third.blogspot.com

For more information on the 33 1/3 series,
visit 33third.blogspot.com.

For a complete list of books in the series,
see the back of this book.

Madness's *One Step Beyond...*

Terry Edwards

continuum

NEW YORK • LONDON

2009

The Continuum International Publishing Group Inc
80 Maiden Lane, New York, NY 10038

The Continuum International Publishing Group Ltd
The Tower Building, 11 York Road, London SE1 7NX

www.continuumbooks.com
33third.blogspot.com

Library of Congress Cataloging-in-Publication Data
The Publisher has applied for CIP data.
ISBN 978-0-8264-2906-3

Typeset by Newgen Imaging Systems Pvt Ltd,
Chennai, India
Printed in Canada

Table of Contents

CONTENTS

Cast of Players

Credits as printed on the back of the album in bold type, additional notes in italics.

Mike Barson (Monsieur Barso)—Keyboards
Also referred to as Barso (without the French title)

Chris Foreman (Chrissy Boy)—Guitar
Also referred to as CJ Foreman

Suggs (Graham McPherson)—Vocals
Suggs is never known as Graham McPherson

Mark Bedford (Bedders)—Bass
Lee "Kix" Thompson—Tenor Sax, Baritone Sax, Vocals
Often referred to as Thommo

Woody Woods Woodgate (Dan Woodgate)—Drums, Percussion
Chas Smash—Backing Vocals, various shouts and fancy footwork
Chas is usually known by his given name, Cathal Smyth

John Hasler—Minder

A Clanger/Alan Winstanley Production
Clive Langer and Alan Winstanley co-produced the album

Recorded at Eden & T.W. Studios

Mixed at Rushent's Mansion (the lucky bleeder) *Alan worked with Martin Rushent a lot, so hired his studio for the final mix*

* * *

They also served…

Dave Robinson—Stiff Records supremo
Also referred to as Robbo

Jerry Dammers—leader of The Specials/Special AKA and founder of Two Tone Records

Prologue

Legend has it that when he was told Ringo Starr was considered the best drummer in the world, John Lennon quipped that he "wasn't even the best drummer in The Beatles." By the same token, *One Step Beyond* isn't the best album in the world—and probably isn't even the best album by Madness, either. It's an important record, though, and is the blueprint for the band's subsequent recorded output. All the fun, pathos, quirky bits of timing, key changes and even an early string arrangement are already in place in their debut album. This winning formula was refined and just kept on winning over the following years.

Once a group reaches the stage that Madness are at now, they have a substantial back catalogue to pick and choose from when they perform live. About 40 percent of *One Step Beyond* remains in the Madness live set, even deep into the Noughties, which speaks volumes about the quality of the early songs and their popularity. If there was no depth to this record, the Madness boat would have sunk under a pile of "Fuck Art, Let's Dance" t-shirts long ago. (Interesting to note here that the f-word appears on the t-shirts, but never in the songs.)

Surprisingly few books have been published about Madness, considering the vast number of records they have sold worldwide over the years. This book is written as a kind of lateral-thinking Rock Family Tree, with *One Step Beyond* as the taproot. Having grown up with *One Step Beyond*, from its release when I was working in a record shop, through recording on Two Tone with my band the Higsons, to working with Bedders, then finally touring with Madness and playing many of the songs from the album, this volume is written as insider and outsider, fan, contemporary and fellow musician.

I am in the extremely fortunate position to have been able to speak to all the major players in the recording of *One Step Beyond*, and these interviews are referred to constantly in the text. I've not written this as an academic tome—there are no footnotes—so I'll state here that the interview with Dave Robinson took place in December 2007 while the interviews with John Hasler, Clive Langer, Alan Winstanley and all seven members of Madness took place between February and June 2008.

The Nutty Train

There's an early photo of the six of us walking down the street—and we just got closer and closer...
—Woody

A photograph taken by Ian Dury of a one-time violinist, then roadie, for Dury's band Kilburn & the High Roads was the inspiration for the Nutty Train, the iconic image that has come to represent the band on several other record sleeves down the line and continues to shift bucketloads of T-shirts every year. The photograph was dubbed 'Paul Hangs Loose' and appeared on the back of the Kilburns' album, *Handsome*, released in 1974. "I don't know who Paul is," says Mike, "but 'Paul Hangs Loose' is what we copied." Paul Tonkin met Ian Dury at Canterbury where they both studied art, and the photo was taken while Paul was jiving along to

Chuck Berry. Tonkin, like fellow Kilburns member Humphrey Ocean, went on to become a successful artist after the demise of the band. Barson, incidentally, was quite taken with some of the artwork that Roger Dean produced for Yes (I know—strange, but true) and Dean also studied at Canterbury from 1961 to 1964.

Woody remembers Mike being very specific about the shape of the arms—"very train-like"—and Mark recalls that they lined up in order of height (left to right, it's Lee, Woody, Chris, Mark, Suggs and Mike). Mike playfully suggests that they were "in order of importance. Lee Thompson at the back. Or in order of the best chance of getting there, most organised at the front, chaotic ones at the back and Chas Smash nowhere to be seen." Having been waiting in the lobby of a hotel on tour with Madness and witnessing Mike order some food at the bar one minute before the coach was due to take us to soundcheck (having had quarter of an hour to make his mind up), I think it's safe to say that his tongue is firmly in his cheek when he suggests he's the most organised. However, Madness was his band first and foremost, and some images of the band (Mike at the front of the Nutty Train and in the centre of the 7 sleeve) are reminiscent of the Rollin' Stones' early press pictures and interviews where Brian Jones was the leader. Once there was a 'G' in Rolling, though, Mick Jagger was more prominent—and Suggs looks like he's breathing pretty hard down Mike's neck! Best not to read too much into that, though, as Mike was considered the best musician in the band at the time, has written dozens of successful tunes and, to date, hasn't been found the wrong way up in a swimming pool.

For the picture sleeve on the "One Step Beyond" single a different shot from the same session was used, this time in colour. It reveals that Mike's wearing red socks (very Peter Cook as the Devil in *Bedazzled*) and Suggs has a fetching burgundy suit on. Woody remembers the session well. "It was taken in a photographic studio in Covent Garden, near where I used to work in the summer. We were clinging onto some sort of rail to stay in that position. The photographer, Cameron McVey, had been my father's assistant at one point." It transpires that Crispian Woodgate, Woody senior, was quite a face about town in the swinging sixties as photographer to the stars in the burgeoning London film industry. He took portraits of actors such as Albert Finney and Ian McKellen, and the Stones' manager Andrew Loog Oldham as well as shooting record sleeves for folk guitarist Davy Graham, including the influential "Folk, blues and beyond…" Yes, it really is 'beyond—dot, dot, dot.' Spooky! Crispian even played himself in the film *Crossplot* (1969) starring Roger Moore.

The Nutty Train can also be caught on the sleeve of the compilation *Utter Madness*, this time with the band travelling right to left, but with Suggs at the head followed by Cathal, Mark, Woody, Chris and Lee, Mike having left at that point. Here the band is in matching 'newspaper' suits and there's a giant shadow behind them. The shadow idea is used again for the sleeve of *Our House*, the Madness musical soundtrack album, but this time it's of the original "One Step Beyond" image, just in silhouette.

You could be forgiven for thinking that Cathal was a last minute addition to the band as he's not on the front cover. In fact he was the first bass player when Mike got the band together (as The Invaders) with Lee, Chris and John Hasler. "I bought a bass for four quid from one of the Hampstead crowd, and played covers in the early days before we did any original material. I had a falling out with Mike over money and left the band," says Cathal. He returned—as Chas Smash—when Lee asked him to come up and introduce the band once they'd got themselves together, so his credit on the album as "backing vocals, various shouts and fancy footwork" is pretty apt. No room for Chas aboard the Nutty Train, then, but there are sixteen shots of him displaying his fancy footwork on the back of the sleeve, these shots being taken by Chris Gabrin, not part of the Cameron McVey session.

* * *

The Nutty Punters

Chris takes the credit for the 'nutty punters'—"It was my idea to get this inner sleeve together, to get all the fans to send in photographs." An advert was placed in the *London Evening Standard* asking Madness fans to send in passport-sized photographs for inclusion in the sleeve, "a lovely idea which went down well with people," says Cathal. The only way to get an instant photo of yourself or your friends in 1979 was either to get a Polaroid camera or jump into a photobooth. The photobooth option was a bit more practical most of the time. At an early BUtterfield 8 gig, when we were supporting Bad Manners at Imperial College, London, Bedders told me that "the photographer was outside." I was a bit puzzled as I didn't know that we were meant to be doing any press. I stepped out of the dressing room into the main hallway, not into the presence of Annie Leibovitz or the like, but face-to-face with a passport photobooth! Some clubs had these machines in them as well. Nothing like a skinful of alcohol to make you want to cram into a booth and document the evening. Lounge Ax in Chicago (sadly closed down in 2002) had a photobooth—the promoter insisted on bands taking a strip of four photos as keepsakes of the gig. It was a precise operation dashing in and out to get headshots of each member of the band. I played there with Tindersticks once and we had to get three groups of two and one 'group' of one in. Wonder who's got that now...

The resultant collage for the *One Step Beyond* sleeve threw up some curious bedfellows—over 150 of them. The band members knew some of the people on it; in fact, Cathal slipped in several pictures of himself, friends and family including Jo, Bernadette, Dermot and Brendan; Bedders is there with Miranda; Michelle Winstanley; Woody, Lee and Chris's wives/girlfriends; Keith and Ben from Smile, the hair salon famous for styling Roxy Music (I was sat next to Keith at the premier of "Our House—the musical," much to my delight); John Hasler's brother Mark, John Rooney, plus Dixie, Ali, Brenda...There's a very young Lee Thompson in there, six columns from the right, three rows up, "wearing my Mum's petrol-blue sheepskin"! That photo was taken at Liverpool Street station, and I recall the photobooth being right next to a "make-your-own-record" booth, too. Thommo doesn't seem to have been tempted, though. Six heads down, three columns from the right was a landscape gardener that both Lee and Suggs knew. "That's Ray," says Lee, "we used to dig up old bottles, spent cartridges and shrapnel on a dump near Finchley. He sold them at the market by Dingwalls" (a famous Camden music venue). Lee's favourite is third from the left, two heads down from the top—a man with his arms crossed, hands on his shoulders with a third hand creeping up from under his shirt...

Quite striking is the Col. Sanders lookalike. "Si Birdsall found several copies of his photo in a skip in Camden," says Bedders. This is before there was any money to be made from dressing up like a 'celebrity,' and God knows how much call there'd be for a Kentucky Fried Chicken body-double, so it must have been a lifestyle choice. Photographer Cameron McVey is in there, two columns from the right and four faces up. Two faces to his left is Chas Smash, looking uncannily like British comedian Al Murray as 'the pub landlord,' a character that would be created over twenty years later.

*   *   *

The big question on everyone's lips, though, is "who is the naked lady with the towel on her head in the centre?"

Dave Robinson: "I dunno—just someone who sent their picture in and wanted to be on the album."

Bedders: "I have no idea."

Chrissy Boy: "The girl in the bath looks familiar—I think Chas might know who she is…"

Woody: "I've no idea."

Lee: "I was told it was my wife, but I'd recognise her bum anywhere. And that ain't it!"

Suggs: "No I don't know."

Mike: "I know who the naked lady is. You'd better ask Cathal about it…"

Cathal: "Nope, I don't know who it is."

* * *

Among those not mentioned so far in the Rogues Gallery on the non-collage side of the inner bag are Prince Nutty—"His real name's John," says Woody, "and he borrowed my motor-bike once, no insurance, no idea how to ride it, and managed to crash it into a car without getting out of first gear…"; Totts and Whets, the 'away' team who used to follow Madness around in the early days (Si, Brendan, Daisy, Kathleen, Kev Campo, Bernie, Oily and James Brown—no, not that one—were the names that Cathal recalled), plus Chalky and Toks who would head-butt each other when the band played "Swan Lake" when not performing general roadying duties. There's a youthful-looking

Clive Langer in there too. And Suggs in a rare group of four—"try to get more than three faces in," he says. "There's a lot of squashing!"

There's a further Ian Dury/Humphrey Ocean link here, though. There's a group photo of Kilburn & the High Roads where Humphrey is holding his voluminous trousers out, a pose that Lee copied for the following LP, *Absolutely*. Ocean made a drawing from the photograph for the sleeve of the "Baggy Trousers" single. He'd made the inner sleeve art for *Wings at the Speed of Sound*, even slipping in caricatures of Ian Dury and another Kilburn as doormen at a Wings gig (we have Lee to thank for this marvellous piece of trivia), but to bring it full circle back to Madness, there was a Chelsea supporter in the Wings crew, one Ian Horne, who ties it all up. Ian worked with McCartney and Wings before being the front of house sound man for Ian Dury and the Blockheads. Via Stiff, Ian got introduced to Madness and has been their sound man ever since, affectionately known as Dad.

*   *   *

So *One Step Beyond* has everything a proper vinyl LP should have in the packaging—lots to look at when you've bought it and you're checking it out on the bus home before you get a chance to put it on. It's all in black and white, very Two Tone, and I'm sure it delighted Robbo that it made it cheaper to print than a full colour sleeve. For all the cool, rude-boy imagery, though, the Nutty Punters gallery is a perfect time-capsule for Camden in 1979. There may be Nutty Girls with "Madness" dyed into their hair and cool dudes with shades, pork-pie hats and thin ties, but there are chaps with 'taches, the odd perm and ques-tionable knitwear lurking on that sleeve. "It sums up the kind of audience that we had," says Suggs. "Some strain of English…not eccentricity, but…not being stupid for the sake of it." Aah, Madness in a nutty-shell. Not being stupid for the sake of it—just primed for the rockiest, rock steady beat of Madness.

Chapter 1—
One Step Beyond...

Thank god for Dave Robinson having the vision to make this the first single on Stiff, otherwise things could have turned out very differently and we'd be sitting here discussing the state of sanitation.

—Suggs

It's the introduction that launched a thousand gigs, parties, radio shows and Madness tribute acts. As you near the venue that Madness is playing there will be gangs of fans reciting "Hey, you, don't watch that—watch this! This is the heavy, heavy monster sound, the nuttiest sound around...," word perfect and rather comforting in its way these days. I'm sure the band would be happy to drop the damn song once in a while, just for a change, or put it somewhere else in the set—The Stones, bless 'em, often play their

perfect set-opener, "Start me up," in the encores—
but "One Step Beyond" remains the Madness calling
card.

How different it might have been, though. In the
early days the band played "One Step Beyond" simply
as a short instrumental introduction to the main set.
Some nights they played the theme from "Hawaii 5'0".
Some nights they played the "Nutty Theme." All were
seen to be a bit throwaway, the "Nutty Theme" seem-
ing to find its rightful place as an additional B-side on
the "One Step Beyond" twelve-inch single. "I thought
'One Step Beyond' was okay," says Woody, "but never
in a million years would we have it as a single. It didn't
represent the band. Suggs wasn't on it."

Stiff Records' boss, Dave Robinson, who had been
discouraged from attending the recording sessions for
fear that he may have too much sway in the proceed-
ings, finally got to hear the finished album at Martin
Rushent's Genetic Studios—referred to on the album
sleeve as Rushent's Mansion (The Lucky Bleeder)—
where Langer and Winstanley had decamped to mix.
He was not best pleased that his live favourite "One
Step Beyond" had been knocked off dismissively,
treated as a filler or a B-side. It was barely 75 seconds
long, for God's sake, and he had BIG ideas for that
song. It was to be Madness's first single for Stiff and
the title of their first album. There were more cards

up his sleeve, however. Robinson knew more about the recording studio than Madness did at that stage as he'd been in the business for a while—he'd cut his teeth as road manager for Jimi Hendrix, among other things—and knew that the length of the track could be altered by duplicating it and splicing it back together.

When the decision had been made to edit the recording to turn it into a single, it was already gone midnight. There was a different mix set up on the desk (and this was before computerised desks with total recall), so Clive and Alan decided that the best plan of action was to make a demonstration tape of how the edits would work, give it to Robinson for approval, then redo it for real. As an indicator of how the sound could be doctored, the duplicated sections of the tape had been put through a harmoniser (an effect that artificially 'thickens' the sound by adding an extra frequency or 'harmony'). It was all very rough and ready. Clive posted the demo through the letter-box at Stiff in the early hours of the morning on his way home and waited for the go-ahead. When he got to talk to Robinson later in the day he was told that the record was already being manufactured from the tape he'd dropped in as they were speaking. Alan was mortified. "It was a quarter-inch tape running at 7½ ips (inches per second)," that is, it wasn't industry standard quality. Too bad—it sounded great in Robbo's opinion and that was that. The end result is a cosy two minutes and nineteen seconds, twenty-five seconds of which is taken up by Chas Smash's introduction.

* * *

Strange . . .

I had a long phone conversation with Cathal Smyth shortly after getting the go-ahead to write this book, during which he told me about a cult sci-fi programme made in the late 1950s, which was the precursor to 'The Twilight Zone.' The series, called 'One Step Beyond,' was peppered with interesting appearances by Warren Beatty, Donald Pleasance, William Shatner, Charles Bronson and Christopher Lee among others, and was, Cathal told me, where Prince Buster had got the title for his ska instrumental. All very interesting, this half-forgotten inspiration for 'The X-Files,' and its completely forgotten sequel 'The Next Step Beyond' . . .

* * *

Chas Smash makes what could be described as a cameo performance on this album. It opens with his evergreen introduction to 'the nuttiest sound around' and closes with the departure of his chipmunks. In between there's the occasional backing vocal plus the written contribution to "Tarzan's Nuts," but he was yet to take up the trumpet, or contribute substantially to the songwriting. Also, his credit for fancy footwork was portrayed on the back cover of the album, there being only six in the Nutty Train on the front. (What *is* this band's fascination with kernels, by the way?) Ironically, it's lead singer Suggs who doesn't appear on the A-side, so it is still a six-piece effort. Equally amusing is that the single peaked in the UK charts at number seven. A numerologist would have had a field day.

"Dave was good at picking songs and having a great strategy," says Mike. "At that time, to choose that song took a great mind." Robbo's success in selecting the band's second hit single meant that they trusted his judgement and this resulted in his having some say in the sequencing of the album. And you can't argue with opening an LP with three A-sides, all of which were top ten hits. In later years, the band scored their only UK number one single (to date, that is...) with "House of Fun." Robinson took it upon himself to direct all the video shoots for Stiff. The Madness ones, highly innovative and a perfect vehicle for seven show-offs framed by a Cecil B DeMille wannabe, nailed the band's image and reputation. Mike Barson would often bash through the latest tune he'd written on the piano while waiting for the next scene to be set up—fairly opportunistic, as the man who held the purse-strings and selected the hits was a captive audience. Robinson's ear was duly bent and the nascent "House of Fun" was chosen as a single at the video shoot preceding sequencing the forthcoming *Greatest Hits* LP. *Complete Madness*, which Stiff was investing hugely in, including TV advertising (small labels simply didn't do that sort of thing), was to have an exclusive new single on it.

Between the video shoot and the recording Madness had revamped the song and what came back was a tune full of verse and middle eight, but no chorus. They were sent back to the studio to record the chorus, which was then edited into the song. This process took a lot longer in the early 1980s than it would in the digital age. Tapes had to be physically cut rather than looped together in a 'non-destructive' edit, plus, at that time, it was extremely rare that a band would play to a uniform click track (effectively a metronome that dictates the precise speed of the music), so there would be subtle differences in tempo between the original and new recordings, even the first verse and the closing bars. Alan Winstanley copied the drum tracks then painstakingly put it all together so that it would work as a song. Suggs had to re-record "Welcome" several times as the beginning of the line began before the edits, so they'd been left with 'elcome to the House of Fun. It can't have been much of a house of fun by the end of the day, but they had at least got a number one single out of it. Armed with that knowledge, have a listen to "House of Fun" and you can hear a reversed piano swell into the choruses under the word 'Welcome,' and they sound a little brighter to me than the rest of the track—which makes it all the more intriguing.

Returning to "One Step Beyond," the joins are harder to hear, but it's a good party game to see if you can second guess where the extra bits were added. Chris Foreman is a little sceptical about how much is repeated and replaced in this song, though, as it's not a very long tune anyway, and there seems to be only one place where the tune turns round on itself. It's easier to hear the join(s) on the seven-inch single rather than the LP or the CD remaster, though—probably because Alan is convinced that he and Clive got their way and remixed and re-edited the track for the album version. And while it's under the microscope, see if you think, like I did, that there's a cow-bell on it. Bedders assures me that although it may sound like one, it is, in fact, Mr Lee Thompson making a 'duck call' noise by removing the mouthpiece from the sax and blowing rhythmically down that bit. It sounds like slap-tonguing, the sort of technique you associate with 'free' improvising players such as John Zorn, but it appeals to anyone with a penchant for mischief or a sense of the comical.

* * *

. . . But Not True

For their short run of Christmas gigs around the UK in 2007 Madness played an intimate opener at London's Astoria in Charing Cross Road. It was the ideal place to try out the brand new digital desk for the front of house mix. Bloody good job, too, as they'd been sold a pup—the state of the art equipment had a terminal fault that couldn't be remedied and sound man Ian Horne had to install a tried and trusted analogue desk in record time before the doors opened. Ian aged visibly, like the David Bowie character in *The Hunger*, that night.

However, there was one hell of a trump card up the Madness sleeve that night. They played the customary encore of their title tune, but with special guest Prince Buster on lead vocals. The Prince—in person! Everyone left with a smile on their face, and it turned a nervy evening into a special one. (The band played very well, by the way—it was just the technology that let the crew down.) Backstage, I saw my opportunity to have a quick chat with the legendary Prince Buster, not to name-drop (well, maybe a bit), but to ask him about "One Step Beyond" and the science-fiction connection. So—"I heard that the title for *One Step Beyond* came from a TV series. Is that true?" "No, man," he said. "It's about getting one step beyond the ghetto, lookin' up, settin' your sights higher than where you are. There's nothin' wrong with bein' in the ghetto, livin' where you live, but you know that you gotta reach out, go one step beyond…"

Coincidentally there's a theory that the word Carribean is a derivation of the phrase "carried beyond," that once you were on the slave ship, you would be "carried beyond the horizon," that is, you'd be transported further from your home than your worst imaginings. It's a powerful image, either way, being carried beyond.

* * *

And so it turns out that "One Step Beyond" has nothing to do with extra-terrestrials—yet if Cathal hadn't told me the story, I'd never have plucked up the courage to ask the song's author how it came about and I'd simply have thought of it as a good old blue-beat knees-up.

Makes you wonder if there's something out there after all…

Chapter 2—My Girl

Mike wrote quite a lot about girls!
—Bedders

"One Step Beyond" may have set the ball rolling, but "My Girl" is the Father, Son and Holy Ghost of the album—Father, because it's a very early song, written by Mike (and even sung by him on the first three-song demo that they recorded at Pathway Studios); Son, because if *One Step Beyond* is Madness in a nutshell, then "My Girl" is bang in the centre of it; and Holy Ghost because, hell, the band's been resurrected several times since Madstock in 1992 and this song has never been out of the set, and is only omitted from Madness hits compilations if it has a note from its Mum and needs a rest...well, you know what I mean.

Elvis Costello, a former Stiff artist, unwittingly provided the musical backbone for "My Girl." Mike

Barson had gone along to the first Stiff Records package tour, which featured Ian Dury and the Blockheads, Nick Lowe, Larry Wallis, Wreckless Eric and Elvis Costello and the Attractions: "When Steve Naïve did a solo on the Vox Continental I was just blown away." Not only that, but he had been working out "Watching the Detectives" and trying to base a song around the opening chord sequence. He wasn't the only one— Noel Davis, guitarist with The Selecter admitted to Mike that he'd ripped off the same two-chord wonder for "Missing Words" (which, to this day, I always think of as "Nissing Words" because there was a typo on the label of a large delivery of them to the record shop I was working in). So Mike thumped away at C sharp minor and A major over and over to wring a song out them and came up with "My Girl"—via several other chords, I'll admit, but this isn't that kind of book (work 'em out for yourself). There's also a bit of a nod to Elvis's producer, Nick Lowe, in that Mike really liked the piano solo in "I Love the Sound of Breaking Glass" and that spiky piano sound gets an airing once in a while on this LP.

Before the band started taking themselves seriously, while they were still called The Invaders, Suggs would often find himself at Stamford Bridge, home of Chelsea Football Club, rather than at rehearsals, so the position of lead singer was often in flux, hence Mike,

Chris, Lee and John Hasler (of whom more later), would share the singing duties. Even when Suggs had pulled his socks up and fronted the band full time, Mike continued to take the lead vocal. "Mike liked singing it," says Chris, matter-of-factly, and Suggs remembers enjoying the spectacle of there being more than one singer, more than one focal point—"I think it added to the show having Mike sing something, then Lee. A nice bit of vaudeville," says Suggs, "something happening all the time." The video, shot in The Dublin Castle in Camden Town, the band's spiritual home, has each member of the band lip-synching a line in the last verse (except, notably, Chas Smash, who sits by the piano, twitching enigmatically throughout, cool-but-hard-but-fair), which gives it that flavour.

Clive Langer recalls hearing "My Girl" at the first Madness rehearsal he attended before taking them into the recording studio, and noting that Mike's voice had a quality to it that was really reminiscent of Robert Wyatt. Unprompted, Suggs made the same observation. "Mike sounded like Robert Wyatt and that's one of the influences on Madness that's gone unnoticed over the years," he says. "Wyatt sang in his own vernacular in the same way that Ian Dury did." The Costello connection continues. After several LPs with Nick Lowe at the helm, Elvis Costello teamed up with Langer and Winstanley. Somewhere along the way Clive had written a melody for Robert Wyatt, a tape of which he gave Elvis for him to write some lyrics. "Something about 'time' was his only instruction," recalls Costello in the sleeve notes to the retrospective compilation, *Girls! Girls! Girls!*. "In a way it was," he continues, "for as I began work on it, the lurid reports of the Falklands war, in the ever-sensitive Australian press, brought to mind this barely futuristic story." And so the heartrendingly wonderful "Shipbuilding" came about, the definitive version being Robert Wyatt's, a Langer-Costello collaboration with Mark Bedford contributing a sublime performance on double bass.

Having heard "My Girl," Clive knew that he was dealing with a band that had legs. "Obviously not a 'fashionable' ska band, or 12-bar covers band," he noted, "they can write pop classics." Just to make sure, he went to see them play at the Acklam Hall in West London, taking with him Glen Matlock, the bassist from the Sex Pistols who had written the lion's share of the music on the classic *Never Mind the Bollocks* album. I've played in Glen's band, The Philistines, a few times over the years and he never tires of telling the story of that night. After the gig, which was a rowdy affair by all accounts, Clive turned to Matlock and asked him what he thought. "I can't hear the songs, Clive," he said, shaking his head. Glen recalls the event with a great deal of humour. "Shows you what I know," he always adds with a big smile on his face. But, to give him his due, he has a great deal of justification in that opinion on one hearing of the nascent Madness set, played in a bunker with a large number of skinheads kicking off every other song (and bear in mind that to be an ex-Sex Pistol in the late 1970s invited some 'enquiring stares' shall we say . . .).

For all the outrage—'the filth and the fury' as the saying goes—surrounding the Sex Pistols, musically they were very much a meat-and-two-veg kind of a band when it came to songwriting and that is largely down to Glen Matlock. His writing was borne out of 1960s stylists such as The Small Faces, and early 1970s songsmiths such as Ronnie Lane where verses, choruses, middle-eights and instrumentals all knew their place. It's the backbone of the Pistols' songs and Matlock is very good at it. For all their sing-a-long, melodic qualities and the fact that we kind of know the Madness tunes on *One Step Beyond* backwards by now, they don't always follow the same formula. Looking through the tracks on their first LP Suggs pointed out to me that a lot of the songs, even the hits, don't really have choruses. Sure enough "My Girl," "Night Boat to Cairo," "The Prince" and "Bed and Breakfast Man" can't be said to have a chorus in them in the traditional sense of the word (just repeating the title over and over doesn't count!), so I'm going to cut Mr Matlock some slack here. Mind you, he could have seen that even without a chorus between them, the songs had something of quality about them, hence his self-deprecating smirk when he tells the story.

Perhaps "My Girl" is such a strong song because you can't put your finger on what makes it so loveable. The upbeat and angular jauntiness of it belies the lyrics that are full of frustration. Clive even thinks the song is funny. "The song defines the poppy Madness sound, everything they typify—the down to earth lyric with a funny twist. I don't know if Mike thought it was funny, but I was amused by it. Still, to a certain extent..." he trails off before refocusing—"God knows how you write an intro like that. It's quite mad." Bedders describes it as "such an important song—the start of everything, really, about writing a pop song." He also observes that it came "almost out of nowhere," but I think it's really a prime example of inspiration being 90 percent perspiration, and although words, music and structure were probably in place from the off it just sounds like Madness, so they must have carefully honed it into 'that Nutty Sound.' Having said that, there is, surprisingly, a dissenting voice in the band... "Not one of my favourites, but the public likes it," says Lee, and he's not one to pull his punches. "I remember not getting inspired by it at all."

Someone outside the band was certainly inspired by it, though. Stiff released "My Girl" as a single on 21 December, 1979 (Stiff by name, Stiff by nature— who the hell releases a record three days before the Christmas holidays when everywhere is shut?), and it did, of course, remain in the UK charts for ten weeks, peaking at number three. David Bowie released his 'sequel' to 1969's "Space Oddity" in the summer of 1980 and it reached number one in August. It's called "Ashes to Ashes." What's the connection? He used Woody's drum beat from "My Girl" and even followed the song structure! No, really, it's true—he delighted in admitting as much to Clive Langer a few years later, and a quick bit of research (okay, laborious bar-counting) shows that the jerky/jaunty skip-rhythm is played in eight-bar phrases in both songs, broken up by ten-bar phrases of a straight rhythm. Songs tend to fall into multiples of four, structurally, so the ten-bar phrase is what adds credence to the story. You'll get into a mess if you try to sing both songs simultaneously, but it's pretty obvious that "My Girl" was rhythmically the inspiration for "Ashes to Ashes," even though the chords aren't the same. Woody's recycled the drum-beat himself once or twice. "Clive gets me to play it uptempo where it becomes 'ska' and slowed down it's kind of Beefhearty ballad," he explains.

*   *   *

"What could've been…" says Mike. "Clive wanted Suggs to sing this and got me to try it lots of different ways, none of which worked, so that he could suggest that Suggs sang it instead. Singing's a funny thing, isn't it?" (Ever the philosopher, Mike.) "You've got to have a good voice, but some people just have a certain tone to their voice that works. Suggs has a certain tone to his voice. Maybe he's not a great technical singer, maybe he is, but he's got a character to his voice…" Alan Winstanley's take on "My Girl" nigh on thirty years later is that it's a great song—"still not sure about the vocal, though." Still, Alan's a sound-recordist and things like decibels, hertz and graphic equalizers tend to cloud his judgement. From my limited experience of working with the band, though, I will say that when we rehearsed songs like "Prospects" and "March of the Gherkins" over and over, Suggs was always right on the money, singing through the middle of the notes. That could be a lifetime and a half of experience, though—he was a fresh-faced eighteen-year-old when he first sang of the woes of his girl being mad at him.

Should you wish to track it down, the demo version of "My Girl" with Mike singing on it appeared on the twelve-inch version of "Return of the Los Palmas Seven" and is available on the CD box-set *The Business*. Barson says "My version's much better," then removes his tongue from his cheek to add, "I haven't listened to my version of that song for ages, and probably don't want to either." Actually, his Wyatt-esque vocal stylings are charming (although they'd work better at a slower tempo) and the song as a work in progress is an education, what with extra bits of percussion and the "sound of breaking glass" piano solo, which was ultimately replaced by the safer, probably more commercial version that we've all become accustomed to. What could've been, indeed.

Chapter 3—Night Boat to Cairo

*I always thought of that song as being an approximation of
what the BBC thought that music from the Eastern world
would be*

—Suggs

This song is a bit of a house of cards as well as being
from the house of fun. The opening fog-horn sound
of Lee's baritone sax certainly conjures up visions of
a pea-souper over the English Channel, but I'm not
sure about the River Nile…and then "it's just gone
monsoon," the monsoon being a seasonal wind that
affects southern Asia, though you'd be hard pushed to
find it troubling the Nile's passage from Lake Victoria
to the Mediterranean Sea. Of course, none of this
matters whatsoever. The video that accompanies this
unlikely top ten single reinforces the colonial imagery. Our gallant lads are all in pith helmets, marching

around a film studio that doesn't have enough sand on the floor to cover the floorboards, has all the props rattling around and some very dodgy backgrounds of the pyramids and so on. You wouldn't believe that the promo was made using cutting-edge technology, the first time they'd shot a 'video' on film, which made editing faster. Robbo is proud of having made it in an afternoon, put it together overnight and aired it the following morning. It all smacks of the BBC sitcom, "It Ain't 'alf Hot, Mum," which was a huge success in the mid-to-late 1970s and was set in colonial India during the Second World War. It is seen now as a product of its time, but nonetheless had a resonance as the class structure upon which it was based was still flourishing. Two of the cast even had a huge spin-off hit single in the UK in 1975, with "Whispering Grass." It was another five years before safari suits troubled the wardrobe assistants at *Top of the Pops* again.

The tenacious Dave Robinson squeezed another single off the album—the first three tracks on side one were the first three Madness singles on Stiff—plus there was the re-recording of "The Prince," also included on side one. There was a lot of argy-bargy about there being yet another single from *One Step Beyond*. Whereas Epic Records had no qualms whatsoever about releasing five singles from one album by Madness's contemporary Michael Jackson (1979/1980 saw practically every track from *Off the Wall* receive a single release either as an A- or a B-side), in the wake of punk it was simply bad form to 'rip off the fans' by making them buy more A-sides from an album they already had, even if the B-side was exclusive to the release. Ironically, in the past ten years the Madness catalogue has been rebranded and reissued with singles compilation after singles compilation, almost King Midas in reverse. A compromise was reached, however, in the guise of a 7" EP, which had "Night Boat to Cairo" as the lead track with not one, not two but three new Madness originals. Extended Play seven-inch forty-fives, as they were known, had been popular in the mid-1960s, but had grown out of fashion. Stiff's third seven-inch release was a pastiche of the famous "With The Beatles" EP, entitled "With The Roogalator." It looked great, but ran at 33 1/3rd and had only two tracks on it. Needless to say, it stiffed.

With Madness, Robbo had the sweet smell of success in his nostrils and he knew that the ska zeitgeist had to be capitalised upon. Whereas "Bed and Breakfast Man" was highly favoured as a single—if there had to be another one at all—the record mogul was acutely aware of the vast amount of sales and airplay that was going the way of The Selecter, The Beat, The Specials and The Bodysnatchers with their new wave of British ska. "Night Boat" was the way to go, he thought, and it was practically all instrumental. He had a passion for Madness instrumentals. Chrissy-Boy confirms this. "Robbo always wanted another instrumental—we were gonna become like The Tornados, just doing instrumentals," he recalls. Strange, then, that Robinson was at pains to point out to me that he'd canvassed heavily for Cathal to be in the band as he was so important to the band's image. Two singers in a group that specialised in instrumentals seems to me to be somewhat extravagant.

Mike had envisaged this as an instrumental, too, and he had the title in place before Suggs presented him with his lyrics. "We used to rehearse at Mike's place in Muswell Hill, and I heard the dulcet tones of "Night Boat to Cairo" coming down the stairs as I was coming up the stairs" is Suggs' picturesque description of the first time he heard the tune. Barson's title evidently sparked off something in him and inspired images of the toothless oarsman and a barely seaworthy vessel. I can't help but think that it's a small step from "Night Boat to Cairo" to "Night Bus to Camden" (okay, okay, it's just over two thousand miles), but the thought of some old chap with a gummy grin that sat on a night bus, the last resort of the homebound drunkard—well, it speaks louder than words in describing all manner of nights out when everything goes wrong that possibly could go wrong, where alcohol and an acute sense of mischief are captaining the barely floating, if not sinking, ship. Actually Chris wryly notes that Suggs had just cottoned on to the fact that you get royalties for writing lyrics; so he turned the instrumental into a song and so turned a profit. Ah, but would it have been a hit without the words? Mr Foreman's being a bit harsh, I reckon.

Suggs describes this as "miles of introduction, a couple of verses then miles of instrumental, no chorus and the title isn't even mentioned apart from me shouting it at the beginning." Yes, Suggs, but it's an excuse to put on a fez and have a bit of a knees-up and you can't put a price on entertainment like that. Sure enough, Suggs' musings on "Night Boat" conclude with "it's an atmosphere with great music and words—of course it IS a song, but not a traditional one." Lee says it's "fantastic" and it gave him a chance to play his baritone sax. "I used to have a silver baritone, cheap, but it had a great, rough old sound to it. It got stolen when I was away on tour in Europe along with some singles." Lee looks a little downcast as he remembers that sax, then the glint returns to his eye—"what goes around comes around," he concludes, tacitly assuming that we all know the story of the dubious provenance of the Selmer Mk VI tenor sax that he first played. (You don't? He bought it off 'a mate' for a hundred quid. There was no serial number on it—mysteriously scratched off somehow—and when the mate realised that he'd let a valuable sax go for a song he tried to prise more money out of Lee. "Sold as seen," Thommo said. End of story.)

At first, far from deeming it 'fantastic,' Mike wasn't best pleased that his jewel of the Nile had become paste in his eyes. "The lyrics made it a bit more trite—I mean, 'just gone noon, half-past monsoon'— it's not very serious, is it? It's nice we wrote the song together, but at the time I didn't rate it. It came over to me as a bit lightweight, a bit jokey, but it turned out all right." Elaborating further, Barson explains that "it's a bit nicked off The Specials. The bass-line's a bit 'Gangsters' and a bit like 'One Step Beyond' so we didn't want to release it." As both of those tunes are haunted once more by the benign ghost of Prince Buster, I guess he has a point, not that I can hear the similarity with "One Step Beyond" all that clearly. Mike was also concerned that Madness might be led down a similar path to another Two Tone-style band Bad Manners (who often get overlooked in reap-praisals of the new wave of ska). "Bad Manners were a good band, but we were wary of the way they were being marketed," he says. At least they were wise to it. Heaven forbid that Thommo might swan (lake) around in a tu-tu...oh, yes, he finally got around to that when he was the wrong side of forty!

"Night Boat" is most notable, though, for the band's first recording with a string section. Langer was very keen to use violins on this track—he's keen to use them whenever he can, frankly—and he talked Madness into letting him use an arranger. Alan Winstanley recalls it being David Rose, though he's not credited on the album and it's highly unlikely that it's the same David Rose who achieved fame and fortune with "The Stripper"...It wasn't the smoothest of introductions to working with outside musicians, but at least it's for humorous reasons rather than anything else. When Clive spoke to the arranger on the phone he asked him to come up with something Egyptian, and he duly did what he was told—except that he thought that Clive had said 'gypsy,' so that's where the frantic, no-holds-barred, break-the-crockery violin lines came from, rather than the enigmatic bare fourths and mystery of the Pharaohs that was expected. Still, there was no time to change boats mid-stream, so everyone went with it. Time was pressing, and in the confines of TW Studios in Fulham the fiddle-players worked away. Once more Alan donned his editing hat and made the end part of the song loop round so that they could get their money's worth. Woody insists that you can hear the track speeding up towards the end of the loop then dropping back into time, but I think you need very keen ears to distinguish the quick beats from the slow as the song fades out.

Alan Winstanley recalls the violins (which Clive describes as "quite frightening!") being kept low in the mix for the album, but they made a bit of a return a few years later when he was asked to do a remix. To make his mark on the new version he made a bit more of a feature of the Egyptian Band of Gypsys and received a phone call from a perplexed Dave Robinson asking where the hell the violins had come from—it transpired that he'd never noticed them before despite insisting upon the track being a single. And this was the man who was supposed to be keen on instrumentals!

So "Night Boat" had come a long way from the Barson family piano in Muswell Hill where Mike would stomp on the floorboards, displacing the dust while he hammered out the chords and crafted the melody, and it has found its place in the hearts of many a Madness fan and is usually the last of the encores at the culmination of the live set. "We used to do the false ending as many as four times," says Suggs. "Thankfully no more." Actually the false ending still comes round once or twice more than intended every now and then when high spirits get the better of everyone, but then, why not? And to clear up the gypsy/Egyptian business, Suggs, as an erudite scholar, mentioned that there was a link between the two words that I should check out. Sure enough, the Collins English dictionary defines gypsies as having migrated northwards from North-Western India from about the ninth century onwards, the definition of the word first being cited in the sixteenth century as being derived from 'Egyptian' as they "were thought to have come originally from Egypt." Perhaps the monsoon migrated with them...

Chapter 4—Believe Me

It's more R+B than ska—it's a bit lazy to call this a ska album because not that many tracks are ska tunes
                                                —Chris Foreman

A couple of years before punk rock slapped everyone in the face there was a burgeoning rock and roll revival and cinema played a large part in it. *That'll Be the Day*, starring David Essex, was the British take on Americana in the early 1960s, but the film that caught the imagination of the soon-to-be members of Madness was *American Graffiti*. The film holds two key memories for Suggs in particular, firstly that it was the first film he'd seen where the music was as much a star as the cast and plot, "the first film I'd seen where the music was at an appropriate volume, not just background music," and secondly that he was asked by John Hasler, shortly after seeing it, to become the singer in The Invaders. The first song they tried out when he 'auditioned' was the Bill Haley and the Comets hit "See You Later, Alligator." Mark name-checks the film as being important, too, and among the wealth of rock and roll and doo-wop classics that permeate the film is Fats Domino's "Ain't That a Shame," Domino being one of the pianists that Mike was busy studying at home, his hit "Blueberry Hill" in particular.

So, with the first three singles out of the way on side one, and therefore about half of the total tunes that could be described as 'ska,' the band's roots started to show—and these particular roots were more American than Jamaican. "Believe Me" was one of the earliest Madness originals, written by John Hasler and Mike Barson. Hasler used to write screeds of stuff, just put words on paper. "Poems, songs, the first two pages of a novel" he says, laughing. "I'd give lyrics to Mike for him to write the music, he'd change a couple of words, then claim he'd written the whole song!" Lee acknowledges that John was the first member of the organisation to write an original. "Quite right, let's stop doing all these covers. We started off doing rock & roll covers," Lee adds. By the time Woody joined the band they were making a fist of it—"This ('Believe Me') and 'Sunshine Voice' were the first songs I ever did with the band."

"Sunshine Voice" and "Rich Girls" are two Hasler originals that various members of the band refer to when discussing their early songs. Neither made it as far as the recording studio. Thommo gave me a brief rendition of one line of the former while Suggs described "Rich Girls" as being about "all those wealthy people we saw walking 'round Hampstead who had fridges the size of which you couldn't imagine!" Given the naïve charm, shall we say, of "Believe Me," perhaps these two songs didn't really cut it, though Hasler's "Mistakes," which was the B-side of "One Step Beyond" is a very fine song and probably just missed being on the LP by a whisker. Too melancholic, perhaps, not the perfect foil for "Tarzan's Nuts" . . .

Initially I thought that "Believe Me" was a good example of the band's Tamla Motown roots, but Bedders points out that it owes quite a lot to 1950s bands such as The Coasters, what with the occasional vocal harmony and the "No-no-no-no" answering phrases in the last couple of verses. Both Suggs and Woody see the early Madness as copyists of certain styles of music, but with their own take on it—and it's not a knowing affectation, but just trying to emulate, say, doo-wop or rhythm and blues, and coming up with something else through not having the expertise to nail it. "Lots of bands at the time did 'pub-rock' versions of the same songs or style of music, but ours was a bit more wonky," comments Suggs. Woody describes his drumming on a lot of this album as being an approximation to a style that, while rarely successful as a believable pastiche, became the spring-board for something else and it was usually more interesting. "For instance, 'Razor Blade Alley'—that was my attempt at jazz drumming; 'Land of Hope and Glory'—my attempt at military drumming in the introduction. I didn't have the technique, but just made it sound the way I thought it should be."

So the resulting track lies somewhere between The Coasters and the Tamla Motown sound. The heavy backbeat on the tambourine is pure Smokey, and the vocal stylings are to be found somewhere in the soundtrack to *American Graffiti*, but the sound is still Madness despite—probably because of—the fact that it could in no way, shape or form be described as a ska song. The magic ingredient to the nutty sound in "Believe Me" is the odd bar or half-bar. The intro-duction has the trademark chirpy piano sound, inter-rupted by the band eagerly coming in on the fourth bar, but only for two beats then landing on the groove. The other trick Monsieur Barson has up his sleeve is that of adding one 'extra' bar to the end of each double verse. I don't want to labour the point here, but with-out these brief deviations from traditional musical form you'd end up with a much straighter and probably less catchy song. I'm not an obsessive/compulsive bar-counter, by the way—I hadn't noticed these little quirks for over twenty-five years of listening to this record and it's only through repetitive playbacks for this book that I twigged what was going on.

When I asked Mike about the odd half-bar and so on, here-and-there, he just said that they felt natural. Perhaps the metre of Hasler's lyrics dictated the structure. Once more there is no proper chorus here, either. We get a couple of verses, a refrain, a verse and then:

"Saxophone!!"

"I wouldn't say that Davey Payne was an influence on Lee," says Barson languorously. "What's the word? Yeah, he used to copy him a lot. In various ways." Yes, Davey Payne was hugely important to Lee both as a player and as an onstage presence. Payne was Ian Dury's right-hand man in both Kilburn & the High Roads and The Blockheads. Let's face it, the saxophone is always a focal point onstage—it looks good, it sounds good (in the right hands, of course) and everyone's fascinated by it. So what do you do when the lead singer is all that and more, as in Dury's case? Well, Davey always dressed to impress, as does Lee in his own inimitable way. Showman Ian Dury told Payne that if he stood stock still during songs when he wasn't playing it would look 'really heavy.' It sure did. I remember being transfixed by the stationary Davey Payne as a wide-eyed eighteen-year-old at Blockheads gigs. Thommo goes the other route to grab the attention onstage by dressing up. So what inspires Mr Lee 'Kix' Thompson? It was interesting that Clive Langer's band got the first mention.

"We saw Deaf School regularly because they were so theatrical. That's what drew me to a lot of bands—Kilburn & the High Roads, Sha-Na-Na, Rocky Sharpe and the Replays. When Madness used to play The Hope and Anchor (a crucial venue on the London pub-rock scene), I used to frisbee out old ska singles and throw pork pies into the audience. I had a tie which lit up, too (unashamedly nicked from the Kilburns). Do something more than just playing music, make it a bit more visual, save the actual music for the records and concentrate on the visuals, that was an integral part." Lee went on to say that he liked people who painted their faces—The Sensational Alex Harvey Band, Split Enz and Alice Cooper all got name-checked. Lee spent a few months in Australia in 2002 and I stood in for him a couple of times on TV shows—well, knelt in for him, actually, as Chrissy-Boy insisted I impersonate Toulouse Lautrec when substituting for Lee as he's a couple of inches shorter than me. On one occasion we were at the BBC and Alice Cooper had the dressing room next door. Had he been there I'm sure Thommo would have been raiding his make-up bag.

Lee's playing style comes from some obvious players, but one or two less obvious ones, too. Rhythm and blues artists of the 1950s were definitely the order of the day, and he listed keyboard players as well as saxophonists as being important to him—"Ben Webster, Gene Ammons, Sonny Stitt, Jimmy McGriff, Ray Charles, Fats Domino. Not Coltrane or Charlie Parker, though, but definitely Ben Webster, that deep and breathy tone." Fabulous though Ben Webster is, it's hard to equate his sound with the Thompson tone. Maybe he never tried to emulate it though. There's also a lot of unnamed ska tenor players whose solos Lee learnt off by heart—mix them up with some stage greasepaint and there you have it.

The saxophone is what's known as a transposing instrument. Without wishing to bore the living daylights out of you, all you need to know is that the written note for most woodwind and brass instruments is rarely the same as the written note on the piano. Much confusion ensues. In the early days, Lee could be playing a tone or semitone out with the rest of the band and he'd try to compensate for this by pulling the mouthpiece almost entirely off the saxophone (that's how you tune it, by adjusting the mouthpiece). When that didn't entirely do the trick he'd try to 'lip' it into the correct key, a technical term for changing the shape of the lips and mouth so that the tuning is affected. All these things make a difference to the tone as well as the tuning and I think that Lee's distinctive tone is a result of his battle with transposition as much as anything. It's a very physical thing, playing a wind instrument, and the way the air's blown into it informs the sound. Just take a look at the way he holds the sax, neck hunched like a heron, bottom lip protruding—that's where the strangulated sound comes from, simply add the metal mouthpiece, whatever reeds he uses (I'm really not going to go down that path!), and you get some way towards the distinctive Thommo sound.

Just one thing to add—I was being quizzed by an eager young guitarist once about what Telecaster I used, amplifier, foot pedals and so on, when Bent Clausen, the leader of the band I was playing in, leant over and said, "I think it's got a lot to do with the person holding the instrument, not what make it is." So to qualify everything I've written earlier, for the record, there'd be no Lee Thompson sound without Lee Thompson. Gawd bless 'im.

* * *

So we go from the sax solo to the bridge, a refrain, a couple more verses, refrain, outro and Bob's your uncle. Mike Barson had successfully moulded John Hasler's tale of earnest endeavour to keep hold of his girlfriend (despite rumours of a scurrilous affair with a girl named Sue) and come up with a loveable gem— with a little help from the 1974 Billy Swann hit "I Can Help," which Mike admitted was the inspiration for the initial chord sequence. Believe me.

Chapter 5—Land of Hope & Glory

He's a pretty good songwriter, Lee. He can get those experiences down on paper. I have the greatest respect for Mister Lee Thompson's songwriting talents

—Mike Barson

Not only did Lee write "Land of Hope & Glory," but he sang it with Suggs getting just one or two lines in. There was never going to be any argument about that, though. As Clive says, "Lee's songs sounded great. They were very much him, and this wasn't going to be a single, so why mess with it? I didn't try to turn it into a pop song or anything like that. It is what it is—Lee's story." And an interesting story it is, too.

Thompson's always been pretty candid about his chequered past, from coyly noting in the sleeve notes to "The Lot" that the song was about a reform school he'd spent some time in "after getting in a spot of trouble" to telling me that it was the best thing that could have happened to him. "I honestly feel that if I hadn't been 'nipped in the bud,' as Suggs puts it, we'd have got into some serious trouble—nothing violent, but just being a pain to the local constabulary," he says. The way he talks about it, you could be forgiven for thinking that it was all a bit of a game, a bit St Trinians versus the local plod (the original films, not the unnecessary recent remake). But for all that, you can see the twinkle dart in and out of Lee's eye as he alludes to the age-old lads' hobby of 'getting into mischief,' and the hard fact that he got split up from his mischief-making buddy. "I used to knock about with this fellow—passed away now, sadly—he was sent to Redhill and I was sent to Chafford, and when he came out I'd started knocking about with Mike and Chris and the chaps from NW5. I decided to go for more kids' stuff, silly bits of shoplifting."

Little did anyone know that two years of the 'stand to attention life' would be the catalyst for a songwriting style that has half-jokingly, but never unwittingly, commented on simple, down-to-earth lives (and deaths) that the other members of Madness are full of admiration for. "Thommo's writing is the benchmark," says Chris. "Cathal and Suggs aspire to his writing." True enough—"Lee has a great imagination and he's good at getting his ideas down successfully," adds Suggs, "And for somebody that I admired as a person, with a rich, colourful past—I could relate to his songwriting."

I guess the great thing about this style of Lee song— and let's not type-cast him as a one-trick pony, as his other songs, such as "The Prince," aren't in the same vein—is that he says what he sees in a matter of fact way, allowing you to make up your own mind about a situation. It's well documented that "Embarrassment," from the second Madness album, is about a family rejecting their daughter for having a mixed race baby, again a true story from Lee's own experience, related in plain English, but in no way dictatorial—a very clever piece of social commentary. Not that he'd like it to be described like that, necessarily.

The song, then, starts with a military-style rat-a-tat that has slightly comic connotations. There was a music hall mainstay called Max Wall who developed a stage character called Professor Wallofski who would strut around the stage to the accompaniment of the same military rhythm. Lee would sometimes do the same during the introduction of "Land of Hope & Glory." It all falls into place when you know that Wall was hugely admired by Ian Dury who had him as a support act on a Blockheads tour and Stiff even released a single by him, "Dream Tobacco," with the Dury penned "England's Glory" on the A-side.

Having got everyone's "Atten-shun!!," there is the roll call. "Bridges. Sharkey. Nutley. Jackson. Thompson." All the names of real boys in his dormitory. "Live we might substitute our names in the roll-call," says Suggs (there's bit of guitar after 'Sharkey,' drums after 'Nutley' and organ after 'Jackson,' as if the band was being introduced), "but Lee insisted that it was the real people on the recording"—honour amongst 'erberts, I suppose.

The mundanity, clock-watching, institution food and the certainty that there was bugger all you could do about it all is neatly itemised in the main two verses of the song. The jaunty middle eight describes the only bit of light relief you could look forward to, watching television with perhaps the only glimpse of a scantily clad female to be broadcast before 9.30 in those days, the dancers, "Pan's People," on *Top Of The Pops*. This is a bit of a nod to the TV sitcom *Porridge*, which starred Ronnie Barker as a prisoner who was worldly wise and accepted his fate as only those who've done a fair bit of time can do. His character, Fletcher, maintained that if you couldn't do the time, don't do the crime, echoed by Thommo's lyric, "Don't complain, learn the game and I'll get through another day." Fletcher spotted a picture of the *Top Of The Pops* dancers in the paper in one episode: "Oh, look at that: Pan's People. Beautiful Babs." Then, wistfully, "Don't know what her name is, though!" (There was, indeed, a member of the troupe called Babs).

"Land of Hope & Glory" was one of the four songs recorded for the band's one and only radio session for John Peel. The Peel sessions, for the uninitiated, were recorded over two four-hour sessions in the course of a day for broadcast exclusively on his show on BBC Radio One. I'm not sure if John felt that the band got all the airtime they needed, so was morally bound to give others more exposure, or if he went off them after the first LP, but the only other BBC session from the period was recorded for Mike Read in early 1980 and featured "My Girl" plus versions of the three non-album tracks from the "Work, Rest and Play" EP. At least two other Stiff bands recorded only one session for Peel, Department S (their session included a version of the hit "Is Vic There?") and, would you believe, Ian Dury and the Blockheads–seems they just can't be separated. Incidentally, Peel's future wife, Sheila Ravenscroft (nee Gilhooly), taught at a North London school in 1969/1970, where one of Madness attended. Everyone's memory is a little hazy, but it's likely to have been Lee. It's also likely that he didn't attend all that often, too!

Recorded after the Pathway sessions and before the album, the Peel version of "Land of Hope & Glory" makes for fascinating listening as it's a work in progress, a demo of the final song. The military tattoo is missing from the introduction and the guitar riff owes more to Dr Feelgood than Ernest Ranglin, plus the intimidatory "I suggest you eat what's given you, even if it doesn't agree with you" section is a spoken voiceover, which works really well. Wonder why that idea got dropped... The middle eight's a bit freer too, with all hands on deck, piano pumping and sax rocking away. Perhaps Clive reigned it in a bit for the LP version, as is his wont.

The great thing for most bands doing Peel sessions was that you were actually getting paid to go into the studio to make demos and get guaranteed nationwide airplay. And you didn't have time to think. "You'd come in from a gig the night before, have only four hours to record and off you'd go. Nothing better than having that total belief in what you're doing— and no idea how to do it any other way," says Suggs. There sure is the sheer bravado of a bunch of young shavers spilling out all over the Peel session, and it's the perfect partner to *One Step Beyond*. (For Madness completists it was released on the Strange Fruit label on both vinyl and CD, and is still reasonably easy to pick up.)

So "Land of Hope & Glory" starts with a rude awakening, "sharp at six-thirty," takes you through the boredom, bad food and badinage you'd expect at a correctional institution, allows you your dream-time (all old lags will tell you that whatever happens 'inside,' they can't stop you dreaming) and spits you out at the end—once more, "sharp at six-thirty." The song dies away and everyone marches off. The outro was intended to sound like hob-nails on a cement floor, to which end nails were thrown over the wooden parquet flooring of the studio with the boys stomping on them. It sounds more like they're tramping over gravel to me—and an expensive floor was given a bit of a seeing to in the process. One last piece of mischief . . .

Chapter 6—The Prince

One of my favourites. I like doing this live. Even now!
                                                —Chris Foreman

Outside of their rapidly growing following, the first thing most of us heard about Madness was their single "The Prince," which was the second release on Jerry Dammers' label, Two Tone. Having hooked up with The Special AKA in the summer of 1979, and realised that they had a lot in common with the post-punk youth of Coventry, Madness struck while the iron was hot. Two of the three songs they'd recorded with Clive Langer as demos for publisher Rob Dicken were certainly good enough to release, holding back "My Girl," for which they had high hopes (and Mark rightly describes as "not Two Tone in any way, shape or form"). A tribute song to Prince Buster, coupled with a cover of the tune of his that they'd named themselves after, was enough to put Madness in a black and white chequered box, and they grabbed the chance.

"Lee was the biggest Prince Buster fan," says Suggs, "he had all the best singles which he kept in a biscuit tin round at his flat." Lee admits to writing it from "bits and pieces of Prince Buster songs, adding me own little touch." His own little touch involved name-checking three songs from every rude-boy's must-have album, *Price Buster's FABulous Hits*, in the first verse (that's "Earthquake," "Freezing up Orange Street" and "Ghost Dance," by the way). Just for good measure—or 'authenticity,' if you will—the sax solo has a familiar ring to it, too. "I was stuck for a solo," says Thommo, "so I played bits of "Texas Hold-Up." It was beginning to look like Two Tone was the record label belonging to 'The Prince Buster Appreciation Society.'

*   *   *

I must confess to being a bit slow on the uptake when the Two Tone bandwagon started rolling. I was born and raised in Hornchurch, Essex, which is on the out-skirts of London. It's commuter-belt East End, two stops from the end of the District Line on the tube and a mere breath away from Dagenham, home of the Ford motor car production line in the UK. Between school and further education, I took a year out, basically to avoid further education in the hope that I'd be discovered by—well, Stiff Records or some-such—and become a pop star. It didn't happen, but in the meantime I worked at Carnival Records in Elm Park, which is one stop nearer London on the District line, a little nearer to Ford Motors and always something of a hotbed of West Ham supporting skinheads. We're not talking 'fashion' skinheads, as Cathal likes to call them, but the ones you read about in the tabloids who chase after you after dark, have some sort of belief in the British Empire and a zero tolerance policy for immigration.

Living in close proximity to such a vociferous minority threw up the dilemma of disliking the fashion, but loving the music. Two Tone had me confused. Dave and Ansell Collins had hits with "Monkey Spanner" and "Double Barrel" in 1971 when I was ten, going on eleven, and I loved every weird and wonderful noise on those records. I had no idea what half the words were (in fact, lyrics have always been secondary to the music to me, but that's my problem), but I'd never heard anything like it before and had no idea how to get to hear stuff like it that wasn't in the charts. No internet back then, and Hornchurch is a very long way from the import shops of Ladbroke Grove. A few years later "Al Capone" by Prince

Buster was a turntable favourite at friends' parties. That blue-beat groove again—nothing else sounded like it, and most of the local youths who were into it were a bit scary.

Fast-forward a couple more years and there I was in the record shop, buying up all the punk and post-punk records I could afford with my staff discount, when John Eley, the Grateful Dead/Van Morrison/Steely Dan loving shop manager made a bulk purchase of seventy-five—yes, seventy-five!—copies of "Gangsters" by the Special A.K.A. This was a bold move, but he knew that the local skins would be in to buy every single copy of anything the new wave of ska could release. How I wish I had a few copies of that first pressing of the first Two Tone record with its collectable paper label for my pension fund…

But when I heard it, I was outraged on Prince Buster's behalf! This was a cover version of the classic "Al Capone" with a few new words and a new song-writing credit. Who were these upstarts with their skinhead following and brazen attitude towards other people's songs? Seems that they were from a similar car-production town, looking down the barrel of a dead-end life, but trying to look up, trying to get 'one step beyond…' "Gangsters" has, of course, become its own song in its own right. I think of it now in the same light as "Independence Anniversary Ska" by The

Skatalites and "Crystal Groove" by The Crystallites, both instrumental covers of Beatles songs by any other name (but don't tell Lennon and McCartney or their publishing company).

*   *   *

There were three versions of "The Prince" recorded in the summer months of 1979, and the album version is the last of them. Between the single version and this was the John Peel session. "I stayed up to listen to John Peel when the session was broadcast (his show in those days was on from 10 pm 'til midnight), and I remember him saying that he thought the session version was better than the single," says Bedders, "which is probably because we'd been playing it for two months longer and were more confident in the studio by then." He also considers the album version to be the weakest as "it doesn't roll like the other two. It just doesn't have the feel." Woody also considers the Peel version to be "the best of the lot."

There appear to be two reasons why the band re-recorded "The Prince" for the album, one being that they were concerned that they were giving the fans their money's worth, so they weren't being sold the same single twice—although Woody says he was glad it was on the album "because the non-single buying members of the public would have missed out"—but secondly because there was the question of ownership. Now that Two Tone had released "The Prince" it seems that Dave Robinson was reluctant to license it back off them, and as it had been a hit, the parent company, Chrysalis, was in a good bargaining position. But it may be that that didn't really enter into it, either, as the sound of the LP version fits in with the other tracks.

Clive Langer regards the first recording to be the definitive version—"Here we developed Mike's trademark piano sound which was derived from Thunderclap Newman via Deaf School. We put the upright piano through a chorus effect to make it more out of tune, more honky-tonk. That became part of Madness's sound for the future without anyone realising it." The Thunderclap Newman reference is interesting—obvious once it's pointed out to you, but I hadn't appreciated it before. Kind of a 'one-hit wonder,' Thunderclap Newman was a vehicle for Speedy Keen, a roadie for The Who, to record some of his songs with Pete Townshend producing, nominally led by pianist Andy Newman. Their hit, "Something in the Air" sounds really fresh today (despite being somewhat over-used in TV adverts) and it's down to the uplifting vocal and remarkable piano solo that appears to have little to do with the song, although the song would be lost without it. Nice baritone sax stabs at the end of the solo—which are echoed, probably not intentionally, in a later Madness song, "Benny Bullfrog." The sound must have registered with Clive back then as he's such a sucker for the baritone sax. Another classic use of honky-tonk piano out of the blue is the solo in John Cale's "Ski Patrol" from the *Slow Dazzle* album (1975), but maybe that's a red herring...

Mike Barson made some changes to the piano part for the album, but doesn't like it as much as the single version. "Don't suppose you noticed, did you?" he asks, and I must admit that any changes to the keyboard parts seem purely cosmetic rather than a radical rethink. What is noticeable about the *One Step Beyond* recording is that it sounds more polished and has a little more intent, even if the 'youthful enthusiasm' of the Two Tone recording isn't entirely there. What picks the song up for me is the percussion—the addition of a cabasa in the sax break, then a cowbell on the last instrumental section. "The band wasn't around for the mixing," says Alan, so Langer and Winstanley took it in turns to play percussion. Chrissy Boy's guitar effects are in full flow here, too. "For the guitar sound we recorded the reverb plate, not the signal," Clive explains, "like some old ska and reggae tunes." What you hear is the 'other-worldly' sound of an echo chamber without the crisp, original sound of the instrument—this effect is at the root of dub, basically. Just turn up the effects, and even put the effect on the effect, making it feed back on itself.

Woody self-deprecatingly says that "The Prince" is "a classic example of me not knowing anything about reggae drumming. I knew nothing about drop-beats (not playing the downbeat, so far as I can work out), so I just came up with something. Even the opening roll doesn't sound right. It's innocent, but it seems to work." Sure does. It's fun, for God's sake! Suggs to the rescue—"it's a good song, even if you don't know who it's about," he says before noting that, once more, Madness had written a hit without a chorus and with a large instrumental section in it. They really seemed to be making a habit of this.

*   *   *

Brian Hewetson, one of the first on the Coventry scene in the Two Tone days with his band The Clique, and a once-upon-a-time Higsons' roadie, got in touch with me just before I started writing this book with a trivia question—"What do Roxy's 'Virginia Plain,' The Cure's 'Just Like Heaven' and

Squeeze's 'Up The Junction' have in common?" I had no idea, so he put me out of my misery by pointing out that they were all UK Top 40 hits where the title is heard once, right at the very end of the song. So, after a year's thinking time, I managed to trump him by telling him that "The Prince" is also in the same category. Shame, then, that the album version puts in a false ending at the expense of singing the title. This puts it in the next trivia category: non-instrumental hits where the title isn't mentioned at all. It's a longer list that includes "Space Oddity," "Unchained Melody," "Parisienne Walkways" and "Bohemian Rhapsody" (the Queen song, not the one by Serious Drinking).

*   *   *

It's worth noting where "The Prince" comes in the running order of the LP at this point. Having kicked off with the surefire winners of the first three Stiff singles, followed by a live favourite and then a Thommo classic album cut—"Land of Hope & Glory" may have been glorious, but there was little hope of hearing it on daytime radio—Robinson picked up the pace and relied upon the familiarity of the band's first hit, albeit in a slightly new guise. "Sequencing an album is so important," says Robbo, "and so many bands blow it." Dave Robinson was in no mood to blow it when it came to the most important band on Stiff Records—he wanted everyone in the mood to dance just before the final word on side one. And there weren't too many words as it was essentially another of Dave Robinson's favoured instrumentals.

Chapter 7—Tarzan's Nuts

> *"Hey you seen Jane?"*
> "No man"
> *"Ok, I'll catch the train"*
> "Train you wait a long time"
> *"No way, I catch a vine..."*
> —"Tarzan's Nuts" (Barson/Smash)

It's not very far to travel from a world where police-men were Keystone Kops, and the petty thieves being pursued were from the old school of Ealing Comedies (complete with accents as unbelievable as their alibis), to the rain forests of *Carry On Up The Jungle* terri-tory. All it takes is a wet weekend sitting in front of the television in 1970s Britain. In the same way that "Night Boat to Cairo" used cod-Egyptian imagery, "Tarzan's Nuts" owes a lot to how teenagers perceived the African jungle—with the help of the television series of "Tarzan." Our parents had grown up with the image of world-class swimmer Johnny Weissmuller as Tarzan, king of the Jungle, up on the silver screen in black and white, but we were glued to the colour TV version starring Ron Ely.

Practically an instrumental with a few lines of banter to kick it all off, it's hardly surprising that these days the band has a very shaky recollection of how the song came about. It boils down to there being two schools of thought. "God only knows what was going on there," says Suggs, recalling the "Have you seen Jane?" lyrics. "It was a funny little bit of instrumental. I'm sure it was taken from a TV theme, but I don't know which one." Chris told me that it was the theme from the Ron Ely "Tarzan" series, adding "Toks and Cathal did the vocals, but we could never get Toks onstage." Lee's memory of the recording is that "everyone was round one mike—I've got a picture somewhere." Mark's take is different—"I get the feeling that Mike had another song in the style of 'One Step Beyond' and 'Night Boat' and it became this very late in the day." Clive Langer goes along with this saying, "I think it was just done for the record, constructed in the studio using various ideas from other tracks. It could have been a Robbo thing, wanting yet another instrumental." Cathal almost disowns it—"I don't know why I'm credited on 'Tarzan.' I had very little to do with this album, I was just on the edge of it." Living on the edge of one step beyond, eh? That conjures an image.

It's left to Mike Barson to shed some light. "It was a bit spur of the moment," he says, agreeing with Mark and Clive. "But where did the tune come from?" I asked. "I thought I wrote it!" says Mike. "I remember writing the middle eight, and it seemed to write itself. It seemed so familiar when I made it up," he says, beginning to look a little worried—'Where there's a hit there's a writ.' as they say—"I'm not sure...Maybe we should leave it that way..." Rest easy, Mike. Aside from the tom-tom drum feel, "Tarzan's Nuts" bears no resemblance whatsoever to the TV theme tune written by Sydney Lee. Mind you, it does sound incredibly like a night boat to Cairo being paddled backwards round Swan Lake—perhaps via Orange Street...

"Tarzan's Nuts" neatly closes side one of the album, though. It mirrors the opening track in that it is largely instrumental, has a Chas Smash introduction and is dragged, kicking and screaming, over the two minute mark by way of a 'live' ending. It's a typical fun track that could easily have been a contender for the B-side of a single; however, it's noteworthy for featuring the first example of the key changes that Madness have used in their songs to this day. "The key change sounds like Clive Langer to me," says

Mark. Lee reckons the key change at the end "sounds like typical Barson. But it could be Clive," he adds. Langer helpfully says that it would be either him or Barson. Mike to the rescue once more—"we'd never heard of a key change before working with Clive, so I think he started off all that sort of thing."

One of Clive's tricks when double-tracking (recording the same instrument twice to make it sound thicker) was to vari-speed the track (alter the running speed of the tape machine) so that the instrument had a slightly different sound quality. Horn sections achieve the same end by slightly detuning their instruments when double-tracking. It stops a phasing effect, too—with Thommo, Alan preferred to trust his Eventide Harmoniser! It could well be that once the tape was spinning a semitone higher for an overdub, it seemed a good idea to keep the key change. Or not. (Just speculating here.) Woody's a bit more down to earth—"If you've only got one riff you've got to use every trick in the book," he says, and sure enough, after the introduction (complete with two false starts) the tune gets played twice followed by the middle eight, once round the tune—KEY CHANGE!!—once round the tune, once round the middle eight, one last tune and the outro. Thank you and good night. It truly is a song of two parts with one change of key to keep you interested.

"We refined it later," says Woody. "Say you wanted to go into a chorus after a middle eight, that chorus would be a semitone down from the others, so if you went up once more you'd just be returning to the original key. Beyond that you could go up again. It seems like you're going up twice, but in fact you've been down once already without anyone noticing." Got that? Don't worry, I won't be asking questions later. Bedders' example of the same idea is that they might kick the chorus up a tone or a tone and a half, then go back down again. "Chris writes like that— 'Our House' is a classic example." It sure is, and it's all very well if you're playing guitar or bass as you can just slide your hand up or down the neck to the new key, but, speaking from experience, "Our House" is a bit of a sod on the sax, trumpet or keyboards as it runs round three keys in the repeated choruses at the end.

Percussion is pretty important on this track and yet again the benign shadow of Kilburn & the High Roads is partly cast over the song. The intro and 'verse' are tom-tom heavy—"I had a load of toms and used as many as I could possibly hit," says Woody—and someone dabbles with a cabasa briefly, but it obviously was a bridge too far and is only heard fleetingly. So it's mainly 'mouth percussion' (you know—the "chukka-tikka" sounds associated with ska, courtesy of Chas) and round woodblocks known as skulls. "I wanted

Madness to use skulls as Ian Dury had," says Clive.
"Suggs had some, then they got lost…" Another set
was found for the recording of "Drip Fed Fred" on
the *Wonderful* album in 1999, though, and Ian Dury
was the guest vocalist on that song. Suggs clattered
away on the skulls like a good 'un. I was delighted
to be involved on "Drip Fed Fred," contributing the
brass arrangement and playing sax on it. Just as the
tune fades out the tenor sax plays a short quote from
the guitar riff of "Razzle in my pocket," the B-side of
Dury's "Sex & Drugs & Rock & Roll" single. It was
the least I could do in homage to my hero. You have to
crank up the stereo to hear it, though.

Madness revisited/rewrote "Tarzan's Nuts" on the
Seven album, according to Mike. "When we did 'The
Opium Eaters' I seem to remember it being connected
to this tune. I think we had to come up with an instrumental really quickly, so we took 'Tarzan's Nuts' and
changed it." I don't know about you, but to me it's
changed out of all recognition. "Once everyone starts
playing it changes quite a lot anyway—that's the wonder of music, innit?" muses Monsieur Barso.

* * *

When discussing the origins of Madness with Clive
Langer, he mentioned how important the visual

aspect of everything was. "They were all great draw-
ers, the band just enlarged what they were in real
life. They all drew cartoon characters." Well, not
quite all, but it was very important from the word go.
Mike and Lee used to go round 'tagging,' long before
Banksy made it bankable. Thommo would sign himself J4 KIX 681—"Just for kicks," and the house
number where he lived (nothing to do with '681, the
burn-up,' a Scapegoats tune that Woody played on
some years later). Woody's signature is something
to behold, an impressive reproduction of the Woody
Woodpecker caricature, Bedders is an exceptional
graphic artist and an incessant doodler to boot, Mike
sketched cartoons from an early age and attended art
college and Suggs would draw reams of cartoons too.
Cathal was never an artist, but was a keen collector of
DC Comics, so the visual side of things was deeply
ingrained. I guess the conclusion I'm drawing here is
that with a wealth of imagery informing everything
Madness does, even their instrumentals conjure up a
vast gallery of 'folk' art.

Incidentally, Madness made a couple of forays into
the world of cartoons worthy of mention. Firstly,
there was the Beano-style comic, "The Nutty Boys"
of which there were a dozen or so issues, the first
having had an over-ambitious print-run of 250,000,
which ended up being given away with some copies of

"Return of the Los Palmas 7," or with tickets to gigs—
but no truth in the rumour that Camden fish and chip
shops had vast supplies of them. Secondly, after Mike
had left and the band began releasing records on their
own Zarjazz imprint via Virgin, Suggs and Cathal put
out the "Mutants in Mega-City One" single as The
Fink Brothers, a DC Comics inspired release.

* * *

And so, back to the music. Once the 'jungle-drums'
had subsided "Tarzan's Nuts" settled down into what
Woody calls his attempt at reggae, half time, off-beat
hi-hats and so on. The tune is completely keyboard-
led, there being no sax solo (just off-beat stabs on
the baritone, even more minimal than the upcom-
ing instrumental on side two, "Swan Lake"), and the
guitar is very back-room, back beat, too. Seems like
the bass is the only instrument on the downbeat. Just
as the attention-grabbing key change is beginning
to wear off (it takes about eight bars), the fairground
organ gets cranked up to save the day in the last middle eight and it's all over bar the shouting. And then
there isn't even any shouting. For all the repetition
of "Nuts-Nut-Nutty" in the first year of Madness's
recording career, it strikes me that while it may have
been a good thing for them to invent their own genre,

'that Nutty Sound' became something of a misnomer, and Suggs has drawn the same conclusion. As we mulled over this track he said, "We used to go on about being nutty, but we weren't a novelty band with big comedy glasses or spotty bow-ties—it was a bit more musical. There was more going on, probably because of our love of music." That's true, but this is one of the more light-weight tracks, I think. Nothing wrong with that, though.

Post-Script

Lee 'Kix' Thompson once tagged the garage door belonging to trad jazz vocalist, columnist, Surrealism expert and bon viveur George Melly—'Good Time George' as he was known. He was absolutely livid and wrote about the event in his national newspaper column, sounding off about what he would do to him if he ever caught J4 KIX. And what was the title of Good Time George's best known album? "Nuts!"

Chapter 8—In the Middle of the Night

Your leg still hurts and you need more shirts—you've got to get back on the road.
　　　　　　　　—Sweet Gene Vincent (Ian Dury)

Most touring musicians will tell you that rock music is all about laundry. Buddy Holly, The Big Bopper and Ritchie Valens died in an aeroplane that was chartered so that they could get to a venue early enough to do their laundry. Brian Eno left Roxy Music because he realised that halfway through a song he was thinking about when/where his laundry would be done rather than thinking about the music. Some bands request new socks and underwear on their rider alongside the vodka, cigarettes, blue M & Ms and so on, to save them the trouble of getting their laundry done—and some venues have washing machines and driers on site so that bands touring in sleeper-coaches can 'wash and go' without having to get the correct change in the local currency.

"In the Middle of the Night" has a slightly different take on laundry, however. The local newsagent, George, a 'nice man' we're informed by the lyrics, takes it upon himself to whip the laundry from your washing-line as you're snuggled up in bed. Quite what you're doing in bed by 8 o'clock in the evening I'm not sure, but that's the way the song goes. The scene is set at the top with the newspaper vendor out on the streets calling out the headlines in the good old-fashioned way, despite George having a corner newspaper shop rather than a newsstand, but let's not let the facts get in the way of a good story—the press never does, and we'll get on to "Don't quote me on that" later...

Lee was sent out into the street in Fulham, just outside TW Studios to be the newspaper man, with Clive Langer revving his van up and honking the horn—not as rhythmically as "Driving in My Car," I'll grant you—to add to the atmosphere. Clive's producer's fee went on a trip to New York to be with Madness on their first visit to the States, all but 800 quid of which he spent on a new van—perhaps he burnt the old one out recording the sound effects for this song. So Lee was out, chuntering in the street to create the atmosphere for the start of the track—and the start of side two, of course—and he remembers a nice old lady coming up to him to see if he was all right! The encounter never made it onto the vinyl, though.

A crisp, bright acoustic guitar—which Clive describes as sounding "a bit synthetic, but interesting"— cuts through the street sounds to introduce the song. As the main character is called George, I can't help but be reminded of ukulele-playing George Formby as this kicks in, but that's my problem and nothing to do with "Madness, The Ukulele Years," a chapter in the band's story that Mark Bedford is trying to initiate as I write. Chris hadn't played much on an acoustic guitar, in fact he didn't own one, so he's playing Alan Winstanley's acoustic here. The guitar's owner was pleasantly surprised, not to say ecstatic, when Chris ultimately got a good take. And Chris wrote the song! Bedders sees this as a typical Chris song—the chord pattern and the way it's strummed has CJ Foreman written all over it. He'd also written the music for an early song "Sunshine Voice," which didn't get past the first hurdle in the studio, possibly because it was musically too similar to this one.

Woody's recollection of this song is quite an eye-opener. "That was the most painful, but most rewarding song I've ever done," he says. "I was a flamboyant player, doing lots of fills and crazy bass drum patterns and Clive made me strip it down to nothing." Mark Bedford adds, "we were playing it much more complicated before—there's a tendency to overplay early on because you don't have the experience." With five instrumentalists and two singers in the band Langer knew that there had to be space to hear everything and "In The Middle of the Night" is a great example of the simple arrangement being for the greater good. The piano enters where a drum fill might be, but as there is none there (in fact, there isn't a drum fill in the whole damn song) you are really made aware of it. Similarly, the first verse is really sparse with lots of dubwise holes in the bass pattern—the baritone sax, rather than the bass, plays on the downbeat—and everything falls into place.

And so to the story. To a man, the band has a collective memory of Suggs getting the idea for the song from a genuine newspaper article about a knicker-thief seeing his own description and photo-fit in the papers and making a dash for it. Not so, however. It transpires that Suggs worked for a time at a newsagents in Clerkenwell, an area of London with a Little Italy enclave (which is getting littler and littler as time goes by), and the proprietor would come by the occasional shipment of water-damaged goods, which he would buy unseen, and try to make a few quid out of whatever was in the damp container. Two such shipments stick out in Suggs' memory, the first being parmesan cheese. We're not talking handy, top-shelf-of-the-fridge packs of grated cheese here, but entire rounds of parmesan, about a foot and a half in diameter, and very heavy to boot. As the young Suggs was going round the local Italian restaurants sell-ing these from atop a flat-bed lorry, one of the slip-pery cheeses (water-damaged and therefore wet) fell from his nerveless grip and went rolling down the Farringdon Road. Whoever found it must have had a hard time convincing everyone that it truly had fallen off the back of a lorry.

The second memorable shipment pertains to the song. One day Suggs saw a huge pile of underwear in the basement of the shop—which could only have come from one of these 'water-damaged' contain-ers, our songwriter is at pains to point out—and the seeds were sown for the song. The corner-shop con-nection was a happy accident. "I feel I must apologise to the family who owned the newsagents because it's nothing to do with them," Suggs told me. "I just liked the idea of the newspaper seller seeing his face in the paper." So the names have been omitted to protect the innocent—makes a change as names usually get falsi-fied to protect the guilty.

"What is it about England?" says Suggs. "Rather than have normal sex-lives, fine wines and dining, we have perversion, greasy macs, etc." (he's referring to Macintosh raincoats here, not hamburgers, by the way). Well, the hobby of thieving underwear crops up elsewhere in British-based songs and cinema. Lee Thompson alerted me to the Roy Ward Baker film *The Anniversary* (1968), in which the matriarch, Bette Davis, presides over a dysfunctional family where the eldest son of three "collects clothes" as he puts it. "I've got a lot of Marks and Spencers," he remarks, by way of innocently explaining away his habit of stealing nylon and lace from washing lines. The year before Pink Floyd had recorded the hit single "Arnold Layne" (produced by Joe Boyd, incidentally, who mentions meeting a very young Chris Foreman once or twice in his autobiography, *White Bicycles*), and Arnold had a strange hobby. That's right, collecting clothes— "moonshine, washing line"—apparently based on a real person this time, who regularly took cloth- ing from off Syd Barrett and Roger Waters mothers' clothes-lines, according to Waters. "Very English subject matter," says Mike Barson. "Why we never made it in America."

"In the Middle of the Night" is yet another Madness song without a chorus, yet another Madness song with a very strong whiff of Ian Dury in it. Dury had songs that he'd call 'shopping list' songs—ideas, one after another, read out as if they were on a list without rhyme or reason. (Except they almost always had rhymes, and the most famous one of which is called "Reasons to Be Cheerful (Part 3).") Okay, so this isn't a shopping list song, but a narrative: it tells a story, almost like a newspaper report, but it isn't hampered by repeating a chorus every other verse just because it's a story told in the format of a chirpy round-the-piano (or uku-lele) knees-up. And that's what gives it longevity, plus you're drawn into the character of George from the off. It takes only half a dozen lines to picture him—a youthful sixty-three-year-old, working class, cheery, self-made man with a sunny disposition. A harmless, loveable rogue . . . And Suggs' succinct use of language is enviable—the precocious sod was only seventeen or eighteen when he wrote this, remember—and slipping in the phrase 'gives your hosiery a fright (and doesn't say pardon)' is a stroke of Dury-esque genius, an Olde-Worlde phrase followed by indignation at hav-ing no manners, not so much as a 'by-your-leave.' The only time we'd have heard the word hosiery in the late 1970s would be in the theme tune for the sitcom *Are You Being Served?*, based in a department store where you could imagine one or two of the older characters having it away with frilly underwear. Well, in a bad dream you might.

Suggs, quite understandably, cites this as his favou-rite tune on the record, since it was the first proper song that he wrote. Lee, though, took it one step further. Not only does he rate this, along with "Night Boat to Cairo," as his favourite lyric (both written by Suggs, interestingly), but he took George's character and fashioned a new song with him as a different kind of pest. "I wanted to keep that character alive, so he went into being a heavy-breather down the public telephone-box receiver," says Lee. "Close Escape" on the follow-up album *Absolutely* begins with George describing his close escape, and how he had to be more discreet with a new, less conspicuous or time-consuming 'hobby.' Again, no chorus, all narrative and a charming, jolly, cheeky-chappy upbeat song with a dark underbelly. Chrissy Boy provided the music once again, and "Close Escape" clatters along with three nuisance calls and yet another mention of laundry. Very classy. Part three of 'nice man George' hasn't materialised yet, but Lee had plans to resurrect him on Madness's seventh album, *Wonderful*—"as a nonce in Notting Hill, maybe," he says, "but it'd have to be comical."

It's hard to imagine 'chatty old George' making a comeback now. He belongs to an innocent age of Carry On films and seaside postcard innuendo, so he's perhaps best left as a memory alongside the "What the butler saw!" machines at the end of the pier—but perhaps that's where he always was. Last words from

Suggs: "This just fitted with the idea of eccentricity, something that's not superficially wacky ('I'm mad, me!'), but has some sort of reality in the darker side of the British psyche. But it's also funny. Comic. Black humour…"

(Oh, and the 'currant bun' referred to is rhyming slang for *The Sun*, a tabloid newspaper.)

Chapter 9—Bed and Breakfast Man

Gary Dovey, one-time Madness drummer and a friend of Bedders, said that John Hasler was known as the Bed & Breakfast Man because he turns up with a voracious appetite. And stays!

—Chris Foreman

Although Hasler's role in Madness is relegated on the *One Step Beyond* sleeve to being their Minder ("Dave Robinson's little joke because I was thin and looked nothing like a heavy," says John), he was a fundamental member of the band from the early days of house-parties at Si Birdsall's place, times when the line-up was in flux right through to negotiating their first deals with 'the industry.' This is the man who could be reached through two or three degrees of separation, let alone six. I wasn't aware of him, yet met his sister Alison in the first weeks of being at University in Norwich in 1979! He seems to have contacts everywhere.

"There were two camps in the band, maybe three," says Mark. "Lee Chris and Mike who all knew John Hasler, the massive link between us all. John was two years above me at school. He also knew Woody who replaced Gary Dovey on drums." John had served as drummer for a while, too, and was lead singer when no one else was there to step up to the mike. Punk had inspired Hasler to get an electric guitar—but no amp, he recalls with amusement—and he used to go to see loads of bands. All the usual suspects: Dr Feelgood, Deaf School, Roogalator, The Kilburns, Graham Parker plus the nascent mod scene including The Purple Hearts and Merton Parkas. Lee, with whom he shared an interest in joy-riding, persuaded him to play drums with Mike, Chris and himself, with Cathal on bass. He got to know Suggs through a girlfriend, and everything began to fall together, fell apart once or twice, then fell together again. John was also on the scene when Guns For Hire became Department S, and there was a brief stint in The Nipple Erectors, the band led by Shane MacGowan and Shanne Bradley.

It seems that Hasler is one of those people that a scene revolves around. He's spoken about with a great deal of affection, too—"John Hasler was great.

I enjoyed John a lot," says Dave Robinson. He is wel-
comed with open arms when Madness travels north
of the border these days (he's settled in Scotland). I
recall seeing the band at Wembley Arena, possibly the
first time they'd played that vast venue, and the lights
picking out John when Suggs introduced "Bed and
Breakfast Man"—"There he is—the bed and breakfast man himself!" he said, John greeting the applause
with a huge grin on his face. But then, while it's great
to have a song written about you ("Listening to The
Higsons"—what a classic!), to be immortalised as a
loafer with no shame, well it's not the kind of reference everyone would cherish. It's another tale of one
of the 'dispossessed' as Suggs says, another outsider
of sorts.

Quite a lot of Madness's subsequent output had
an element of pathos to it. It's fitting, then, that
Mike reveals that he was "trying to rip off 'Tears
of a Clown,' would you believe?" Mark remembers
a different Motown influence. "I think this started
off as 'Ain't Too Proud to Beg,'" he says. "The bass
moves more than the chord sequences. The drums are
straight, but the bass bubbles along, trying to kick it
along." Suggs takes some sort of pride in pointing out
that yet again this is a song with no real chorus. "It
went: verse; instrumental; verse; instrumental; middle
eight—with no choruses, no key change, no nothing.

It's the same meter for every verse, just a really simple song about someone who comes round and eats stuff out of your fridge!" he says.

Sure enough it has a simplicity to it, but the devil's in the detail. It divides neatly into four-line verses broken up by instrumental half verses, reminding me of the time that Bedders played me the early demo of "Driving in My Car." That song has four-line verses with an instrumental line between each sung line. The original demo had all four lines sung without interruption followed by the same length instrumentally. It makes for a totally different song and is certainly not as catchy. The hooks in "Bed and Breakfast Man," though, are the instrumentals either side of the middle eight—they each have an extra bar and a half added, making the climax that bit special, and the middle eight itself is an example of lifting the key a tone and a half, then letting it settle back into the original key of the verse. Looks like the band were on to a winning formula very early on.

Clive Langer describes the song as "dead solid, a great song. Barson comes up with something in a melody that no-one else does. And he writes a great mundane lyric." Certainly it has the stamp of Mike Barson all over it, but there's a dissenting voice about the origins of the song. "I wrote a lot of the lyrics—which Barso disputes—and it's a shame, really, because in the entire Madness catalogue there is no song which I've written with Mike," says Chris. To add to the speculation of authorship, it's well-known that Chris always sang this song live in the early days. He even sang it on the John Peel session and one of the band's first reviews has a photograph of Madness at the Dublin Castle with Chris in full voice—and Suggs on guitar! "I tuned the guitar so that Suggs could play it with one finger on that tune while I sang it," Foreman explains, "but when we got in the studio Clive wanted Suggs to sing it, which is right, really." Mike's memory of the origins of "Bed and Breakfast Man" is that he wrote it in his Morris 1000 van when he had a delivery job. "It came pretty easily. I wrote it in an hour when I was doing my rounds."

It's interesting that Chris and Mike don't have a co-authoring credit. All the main songwriters in the band have their own strengths, and they do seem to cross-pollinate a little as writers, but perhaps, "Bed and Breakfast Man" aside, Mike and Chris may simply not be on the same wavelength when it comes to writing. Mike admits, "I remember Chris having the chords to 'Our House' and I thought it was going nowhere. The chords didn't work as a song—we had a little rhythm going, and it was sounding all right, but then Cathal sang the melody and I thought—'I didn't see that coming!'". He can be a bit self-effacing when discussing his songs. Having the same jolly-up from John Hasler as Suggs did—"that looks easy enough, and if he can do it, I can"—Barson set about writing songs "a bit like punk-rock." He reasoned that if there was no fence to climb over if you were playing in a punk band, no level of proficiency to aspire to, then songwriting could be approached in the same way: "If you could play anything, then you could write anything." He goes on to say that "if there'd been a great songwriter in the band, a 'Ray Davies,' then I probably wouldn't have written a song because of feeling inhibited, trying to compete." Between them, the Magnificent Seven have created an output worthy of a couple of Ray Davies's, I reckon.

*　*　*

Having got his place in the hearts of all Madness fans as the "Bed and Breakfast Man," it's worth noting what John Hasler did for the band behind the scenes as it all took off. Having got everyone together—not exactly a manufactured band in the style of The Monkees or the Spice Girls, I'll grant you—he seemed to find his niche in the back-room. Hasler says that no one was trusted to look after the money they'd earned from gigs, so he became the manager. He worked out of the Two Tone and Specials managers' offices for a while, perfectly amicably, but Stiff seemed to view them as "the competition" and insisted he move out. Sounds a little like Blur versus Oasis or Rods 'n' Mockers to me, but Robinson knew what he wanted from the Madness organisation and, occasionally, he got it. He also managed to talk the band into getting new management a short while later, but not before Hasler had helped negotiate a strong deal, keeping the UK and US agreements separate and holding out for a favourable percentage of record sales, and was involved in drawing up the contract for publishing their own material (which is more lucrative than record sales on the whole). He kept his sense of humour while he was doing business, though—he put calls through to Dave Robinson's secretary in the midst of negotiations pretending to be Mickie Most, whose RAK label had been in contention for signing Madness. Highly unlikely that it bothered Robbo, but full marks for trying.

*   *   *

Always a live favourite, and considered nowadays a jewel of an album track, "Bed and Breakfast Man" is, in fact, the single-that-never-was. Alan Winstanley always thought it should have been a single and Clive Langer describes it as "one of the best-known and loved Madness tracks." Suggs explains that the band thought it would be the first single off the album, which was why they made a video for it and tacked a hook-line on at the end. "It hasn't really got a chorus, so we made up the bit at the end (repeating the title over and over), which I don't think Mike really liked." Describing it as "the football bit," Suggs also says that before playing with Madness the only time he had ever sung in public in his life was at football games— "and I don't think that counts!"

The video for "Bed and Breakfast Man" was mainly shot at the Clarendon Ballroom in Hammersmith. Lee explained that this had been the venue for Dave Robinson's wedding party, which he booked Madness to play prior to signing them because there was no other way he could get to see this hot band before his honeymoon. "I don't think my wife has ever forgiven me," Robbo says. Still, the location wasn't chosen for sentimental reasons, but because there was a black-and-white chequered carpet all over the place that suited the new wave of ska. The problem was that the song didn't suit the new wave of ska. "It doesn't make sense calling us a ska band when we did songs like this right from the beginning, songs with a regular back-beat," says Woody. "There're a lot of bass drum beats in this. You could take this beat and put an AC/DC song to it. There was no correlation between what I was playing and ska right up until we did the Dangermen sessions," he says. Hmmm. Discuss...

"It was what we were at the time—really simple," says Suggs, summing it all up, and you know he doesn't mean it like *that*, but the song really is quite simple. It drives away with the inventive bass-line leading the rhythm section, and Clive drops a tambourine in a couple of times to keep things rolling along. It's a story of an ordinary chap, made good at the occasional expense of someone else's groceries, a cheeky chappy and a good excuse to find out a bit more about the man who kickstarted Madness. Nice to know that he liked to keep outsiders guessing, though. "At the first Madness rehearsal I went to," Clive tells me quietly, "John Hasler was repeatedly throwing a flick-knife into a pillar. I thought it was a bit weird."

Chapter 10—Razor Blade Alley

The song isn't about what the title says! A wacky old lyric along the same lines as "House of Fun" and "Pac-a-mac". Safe-sex songs…

—Lee

Given the skinhead following of the Two Tone bands, if you were to go on the song title alone you'd be forgiven for thinking that "Razor Blade Alley" was a song of senseless violence meted out by the likes of the 'The Mile End Mob,' 'The Inter City Firm' or some such football-related hoodlums. It's actually about getting a dose of venereal disease, a taboo subject at the best of times, but in the 1970s the only information you got about it—certainly as an impressionable, inexperienced teenager—was by Chinese whispers and strange little 'Information' stickers in public toilets with telephone help-lines printed on them. The first British 'Public Information Film' related to sexually transmitted diseases was aired on television in 1987 with the catchy line "AIDS—don't die of ignorance!" Seems it was still okay to be ignorant of 'lesser' STDs.

Aside from *American Graffiti*, there was a different film that was to inspire a couple of songs on *One Step Beyond*: an influential coming-of-age movie set during the Vietnam War. "The razor blade bit came from a film called *The Boys in Company C* (1978)," Lee explains, "and that's how I started the song—from the line in it where the G.I. gets a dose of the clap and says 'I feel like I'm pissing razor blades.' That stuck in my mind." While it was okay to put Lee's tale of a loveable ne'er-do-well among the singles on side one, Dave Robinson dropped "Razor Blade Alley" into side two with the knicker thief and the drop-out who 'never liked his Dad.' "Very strong social comment in his songs," Robbo says (but goes no further).

Mike describes one of Thommo's songwriting processes like this: "Lee would write lyrics to other records and then we'd make up another tune round it." I seem to remember reading that David Bowie and Iggy Pop used much the same method for some of the songs on *Lust for Life*. Barson continues, "I remember him showing me the piano part for this—he wrote all the parts. I don't know if what we ended up with was what he envisaged, but he had a clear idea of the whole song." It seems that the bass-line was a bit more elastic, however. It rolls around the vocal in places and drives Woody's "attempt at playing jazz" in the middle section—and that precocious whipper-snapper, Bedders, was barely eighteen years old when this album was recorded. Mark says that "Land of Hope & Glory" and "Razor Blade Alley" are "very worldly songs, which were beyond me at that time as I was younger." Fair enough, but it just goes to show the class of both the songwriting and the playing that it all holds up so well thirty years later.

The bass sound itself is worth a bit of investigation. Until you start listening out for it, you hardly notice what the bass is doing. It's often said of jazz guitarist Jim Hall—and I believe he started the rumour—that his contribution was 'to make everyone else sound good.' It may seem to be a very damning thing to say about a musician until you realise just how bloody hard it is to do that. The growling introduction to "Our House" is Bedders' trademark sound, but it has always been there, and is particularly noticeable on "Razor Blade Alley." Alan Winstanley had started off recording bands such as The Stranglers, Generation X and 999 in the basement studio at T.W. in Fulham. Stranglers bass-man Jean-Jacques Burnel had a unique sound, which Winstanley engineered.

"The '(Get a) Grip (on Yourself)' sound was a fluke," says Alan. "The speaker blew and it sounded good, so they manufactured the same 'blown' sound later with a proper speaker." Clive fills in the gaps—"There was an Ampeg, Portaflex bass amp at T.W. where Alan had recorded The Stranglers. You put a Fender bass through it and it sounded great. Mark's sound is just less distorted than The Stranglers' sound."

"Razor Blade Alley" is one of the songs that Mike lists, alongside "Believe Me," "Land of Hope & Glory," "Middle of the Night" and "Bed and Breakfast Man," as examples of non-ska songs on *One Step Beyond*, showing their mid-1970s roots, rather than the punk and New Wave influence. Chris Foreman mentioned Alex Harvey as an unlikely early influence on Madness, which brings to mind Harvey's rendition of the Jacques Brel song "Next," about a raw recruit to the army standing in line "at a mobile army whore-house, a gift of the army—free of course," hoping that he wouldn't be pissing razor blades the next day. Chris also noted that as Lee was singing, Suggs got to play the organ on this at gigs.

"I used to play the organ on this live as Mike couldn't do both piano and organ on that song," says Suggs (though I'm sure they just gave him something to do to keep him out of trouble). "Another great lyric from Lee which he used to sing live," Suggs continues.

"He got so nervous about singing he'd have his hands behind his back, and you could put a clave [a percussion instrument, one of a pair] in his hand and he wouldn't notice it. He'd just grip onto it and not let go." These days you just can't imagine Lee "Kix" Thompson being the shy, retiring type, delivering his songs like a rabbit stuck in the headlights. A few months before Madness staged their reunion shows at Finsbury Park, Bedders persuaded me to play a couple of shows at Camden's Dublin Castle to promote a twelve-inch EP we'd recorded called "Terry Edwards Salutes the Magic of The Fall." Chrissy Boy had been on the record and he got Lee involved, so we had three members of Madness onstage playing ska covers and Fall songs for fun—and Lee got us to play "Razor Blade Alley," too. Had I known about his 'hands-behind-backs' singing style, I'd have slipped a stick of rhubarb in his chubby little mitts.

Once you take a look at the lyrics you can see the thread running through what Lee describes as his 'safe-sex songs.' Seems that he likes to slip in an advert for using a condom on every other album...He mentions "Pac-a-Mac" from *Seven* which has thinly veiled references to the unborn, a 'small chap / tall chap,' a rubber wall and so on—it's not too difficult to piece it all together. "House of Fun" isn't too obvious at first, with the 'pack of party poppers that pop in the night'

TERRY EDWARDS

getting past the officious censors at daytime radio in Britain, but of the three safe-sex songs, "Razor Blade Alley" certainly tells a grim salutary tale rather than a snigger-behind-your-hand joke. I quite like the line "Felt like a knight without shining armour on at the time" as it reminds me of the junior at a famous West End press office who was a little out of his league looking after some of the well-established clients. On meeting Moody Blues singer Justin Hayward, he asked, "I've always wanted to know about 'Knights in White Satin'—does that mean that you're wearing a condom? Is that what your knight in white satin is?" I don't think he lasted more than a few months at the press office. Hayward's reply went unrecorded.

*　*　*

As with a lot of Lee's songs there's a more than fair bit of Ian Dury's influence in "Razor Blade Alley," the instrumental section in particular. The semi-intelligible mutterings are highly reminiscent of "Clever Trevor" from *New Boots and Panties!!*, so much so that you half expect Thommo to explain to you that "it takes much longer to get up North—the slow way..." The song isn't delivered in Dury's style—that half-sung/half-spoken approach—but the melody has barely three notes to it. As Ian liked to say that he 'couldn't carry a tune in a bucket' he'd have liked the one-note samba (without the samba) of "Razor." The song tells a linear story and, guess what? There's no chorus! And Suggs didn't even point it out to me. Maybe he wanted me to discover it for myself.

There's certainly a live feel to this track—not that it sounds like any of the music on *One Step Beyond* was drilled into the ground in the studio—and Mark says "I've a feeling I was playing along with the vocal. A bass figure mimics the singing [he 'doubles' the title with Lee just after the instrumental section], so either they used the guide vocal for real or replicated it." What he means is that when the core members of the band record a track all together the singer often performs along with them so that everyone knows where they are in the song, and also to get the feel right, but there is no intention of keeping the vocal performance as it's just a guide for future overdubs. Once in a blue moon the guide vocal is kept for the final mix if it's considered good enough.

"The song almost falls apart on a couple of occasions," Mark continues, and you can, indeed, hear a very rare slip of the finger on the piano riff at one point, which adds credence to the idea that the majority of the track was recorded live and kept with very few overdubs. There's just one piano track and one organ track (often Barson added several keyboard parts), very minimal guitar, no saxophone, no backing vocals and a couple of hints of percussion—including something sounding like two sticks being rubbed together giving a very rudimentary vibe of a razor strop, not that anyone under forty knows what a razor strop is anyway. And despite—no, because of—the minimalism, Bedders says "I think it's a great song. It sounds really strong still." Time for some advice from the Suggs School of Record Production—"Simple records without too many overdubs sound great because each sound has its own space. When you've got layer upon layer it makes life difficult—you spend hours on a sound you know will get buried in the mix anyway. Just get the whole track up and see what it sounds like." As I was speaking to Suggs in the spring of 2008, during the recording sessions for *The Liberty of Norton Folgate*, their first studio album of original material for some years, I think he was reminding himself of the freshness of *One Step Beyond* in comparison to, say, *Mad Not Mad*, an LP of very good songs suffocated by mid-1980s technology.

"Razor Blade Alley" is one of Lee's crowning glories, then, and unlike every other track on *One Step Beyond* (with the exception of the a cappella closing track) it's completely saxophone free. Interesting that "The Boys From Company C"—Tagline: "To keep their sanity in an insane war, they had to be crazy"—also had a bit of a hand in the US Marines chant of "Chipmunks Are Go"—but more of that later. Sax and conscription obviously don't mix. Also funny that Thommo was a little more sheepish when talking about the 'safe-sex' songs than his time at Chafford. At first he shrugged off "Razor Blade Alley" by saying, "I don't know how that came about—I've got a thing about fleshy bits and diseases!" But we know different now, don't we?

Chapter 11—Swan Lake

I remember going to see bands with Mike and you could never hear the keyboards—but it's such an important part of Madness

—Chris

"**S**wan Lake" is one of four cover versions on *One Step Beyond* and it is, to all intents and purposes, a cover of a cover. "A straight ahead copy of The Cats' version," says Mark. The Cats released a handful of singles from 1968 to 1970, the first being a reggae version of "Swan Lake" and the second happened to be a cover of "My Girl"—obviously not the Madness song, but an amusing coincidence. Another 'strange-but-true' tale is that when Bedders and I started playing music together, a year after Madness and The Higsons, our respective bands, had split up, we secured a recording deal with Go! Discs, but had no name for the band. The label's main man, Andy MacDonald, who had worked as press officer for Stiff at one point, suggested we call ourselves The Cats—"you know, like 'cool cats,' a respectful group of musicians…" Thankfully, we called ourselves BUtterfield 8. I think we'd have rather been 'Edders & Bedders' if the label had insisted we have a throwaway name.

Suggs used to pick up singles on the Blue Beat and Trojan labels in the early 1970s. "My Mum worked in Soho for most of her life," he says, "and I lived in and around there. There was a stall in Berwick Street market which had loads of Blue Beat singles, and that's how I started getting into that music. I liked the covers and I liked the label." The Cats' version of "Swan Lake," although it was on Trojan rather than Blue Beat (catalogue number BAF 1, fact fans), must have been known to him from that time. "I loved that song," says Suggs, "but I don't remember whose idea it was to cover it. This song always had a sort of magic for me." Mike Barson remembers Paul Chisholm, a friend of his brother, having this record. As it's piano-led it seems more than likely that it was Mike's idea, and he'd have spent some time playing the record over and over to learn it. And although it's a pretty straight rendition of the original, it has the Madness stamp on it.

"I don't remember that much about it except that I enjoyed recording it," say Clive. "It was Madness, rather than trying to emulate the ska sound." Certainly the guitar takes more of a backseat here, allowing the keyboards plenty of room to lead from the front. Clive again: "We had the English poppy sound which came through all of us playing in New Wave and punky bands." Coupled with Alan Winstanley's expertise in recording some of the New Wave of British bands, alongside producer Martin Rushent, they certainly managed to capture the zeitgeist, remaking/remodelling music from the previous decade, but empowering it with what Woody describes as "completely fresh, a fantastic, innocent, raw sound. The magic of the album is that it's played by kids." Who'd have thought that just a few years after the chart return of "Nutrocker" by B Bumble and the Stingers (let's gloss over the fact that ELP also covered that...), Madness could breathe life into another pop version of a Tchaikovsky tune? "Trying to do a beat to a classical song isn't that easy," Woody continues. "I made a right cock-up, but fortunately Clive kept it. It was a mistake which seemed to work." It works so well that I can't really hear what he's on about, but I think it's the dropped beat just before the minute mark where the sax comes in. Maybe Woody discovered what the reggae drop-beat was all about in this song—and he did it by losing his place, but keeping going for the greater good.

* * *

Madness's choice of cover versions can be revealing. Naturally when bands or artists start off, they often play other peoples' music. The vast majority of debut albums in the 1960s and 1970s included cover versions of songs by The Beatles, Bob Dylan and The Rolling Stones to every single outfit from the British Blues explosion. And, given a few years to look back on them, it's pretty interesting to see where they all came from. Madness, with all their youthful enthusiasm and hearts proudly displayed on their sleeves, presented four cover versions on *One Step Beyond*. However, the following albums, *Absolutely*, *Seven*, *The Rise & Fall* and *Keep Moving*, were entirely self-written affairs. In the midst of those releases, though, was one of the band's best known and loved singles "It Must Be Love." This Labi Siffre song was refashioned to such a degree that it's almost rewritten and, like a stick of rock, has "Madness" written all the way through it. Siffre must know how Bob Dylan felt when he heard Jimi Hendrix's version of "All Along the Watchtower." Bedders recalls that "Mike always liked 'It Must Be Love.' Woody and I did most of the arrangement, though. Clive sorted the pizzicato strings. Our style was so well developed by then [1981] that it just fell into place".

Quite often the 'serious artiste' would release self-penned albums, but allow a well-loved cover version or two to appear as a B-side or additional track on a single. Madness didn't even do that. Most of their B-sides were also originals. It helps having several songwriters in the band, all vying for their place on albums and singles, and they're all reasonably prolific to a greater or lesser extent. Madness can pride themselves on a higher than average mark of quality control with their output, too. Rarely did any old rubbish get slipped on to a B-side and, in a time of multi-format releases (a single could count towards chart sales as a 7", 12", picture disc, etc.), that's a fair achievement.

When it came to recording *Mad Not Mad* (that 'difficult' sixth album) Madness opted to record a cover that was to become a single. "The Sweetest Girl" had been, if not a turntable hit, then an indie/student disco classic—well, at least the soundtrack to a lot of head-scratching in bedsits up and down the country. The plaintive sound of Scritti Politti's signature tune was the opening track on the *New Musical Express*'s giveaway cassette (yes, cassette—it was 1981) compiling the great and the good associated with the Rough Trade label. Everyone knew the song, and on paper it was an inspired choice for Madness to cover. My pal Frog, from the Suffolk band The Farmers Boys, told me he'd heard it just ahead of the release. "What's it like?" I asked. "It's like Madness doing 'The Sweetest Girl,'" he said, and he was completely right. For once Madness had almost been 'wacky' rather than 'nutty,' and it didn't quite work. Actually, I don't think that this cover is that bad at all—it's just that the bar had been set so high by the covers on *One Step Beyond* and *It Must Be Love* that it's easy, if churlish, to feel short-changed.

A few years into the twenty-first century, Madness embarked upon a covers album. By this time I'd played with the band a few times and I attended the first couple of rehearsals. We'd played "It Mek," "Israelites," "Wonderful World (Beautiful People)" and "Bright Lights, Big City" during the 2003 Christmas tour, then tried "Phoenix City," "Shame & Scandal," "Crying Over You" and the theme from "Danger Man" in rehearsal. At this point I had an impossible diary-clash, which meant that I couldn't continue with what were to become The Dangermen Sessions. Having heard that Roxy Music's "The Bogus Man" had been demoed, I'd hoped that the cover's album, which was in the pipeline, would steer away from the tried and tested (I mean, two really obvious Desmond Dekker tunes, for gawd sakes), but I think the resultant album, *The Dangermen Sessions Volume One*, stands as a missed opportunity. I'd quite like to appoint Robyn Hitchcock as 'Honorary Selector of The Cover Version' for Madness. In 2007 Hitchcock recreated Pink Floyd's "Games for May" concert at the Southbank Centre in London. Woody was guest drummer for half of the event, and Robyn had said how he'd always thought that Madness could do a great version of "Bike"—go on, close your eyes and imagine the band re-inventing Syd Barrett's perfect pop song. After all, they're kindred spirits through the "Arnold Layne"/"In the Middle of the Night" connection...

* * *

"Swan Lake," however, "was a cover we did right from the very beginning," says Woody. "That and 'Hawaii 5'0.' We used to open with 'Hawaii 5'0,' actually, and I can't remember if we recorded it for *One Step Beyond* and didn't use it." Chris notes that they still play "Swan Lake" occasionally. I guess that one big difference is that Chalky and Toks no longer get up to playfully head-butt each other in time to the off-beat stabs in the middle eight. The Cats' original version has a flute solo towards the end, which I mentioned to Thommo who said, "I did have a flute, but didn't have a clue how to play it, so I just settled for some baritone stabs." A wise move. "I'm a big fan of baritone sax," says Clive. "I always like to get Lee to double other parts like piano lines on the baritone." Thommo was absent for one recording session where I led the horn section for "Wonderful" where Clive got me to play a single low baritone note just once, the sort of event that makes an arrangement come to life, a great example of what makes a Clanger/Winstanley production stand out from the rest.

There had been talk of this being yet another single. Chris wasn't joking when he said that Dave Robinson saw Madness as The Tornados of the 1970s ska-revival (though you wonder who was the Joe Meek and who was Heinz…). Lee remembers that they'd even got as far as pressing up some white label advance copies, "which Stiff called 12" Hot Biscuits." Amusing, then, that Thommo put a box away under his bed, next to the biscuit tin that housed his 7" singles. Suggs tells me there was a second biscuit tin at Lee's place that was full of two pence pieces (the coins that phone-boxes would have been full of in those days, but let's not dwell on that) and he promises to pay back the twelve pence he took from it shortly after *One Step Beyond* was out—he just wanted that on record in this book!!

It seems that the members of Madness who played on this track don't remember too much about the recording session. Suggs says that he thinks he played claves on it, but he must have left them in Lee's hands during "Razor Blade Alley" as the only percussion to be heard is some woodblocks (possibly skulls) that it's highly likely that he did play—Clive Langer remembers Suggs being around for throughout the whole album "and was really interested in the recording process" so he'd have been on hand for the odd bits of 'fairy dust' that need sprinkling over the tapes during the mixing process.

Despite being poles apart from "Razor Blade Alley" in that "Swan Lake" is short and good-humoured, rather than lightweight, the two tracks sit well together on the album, probably because they're recorded sparingly. Again there's just bass, drums, one guitar, two keyboard tracks and some percussion. The baritone sax provides highlights here where there was a vocal on the preceding track, but you can definitely see that Dave Robinson's track order was following a winning formula. I've no doubt that Clive Langer had some input to the final running order, but Robbo held the reins.

Chapter 12—Rockin' in A*b*

There's not much I can say about "Rockin' in A flat." I'd left the band by then. I know it was written by Bill Smith AKA Upright Willie Wurlitzer. I think Bazooka Joe and it's many incarnations was quite an influential band. It's a shame we/they didn't get to make any records.
— John Ellis, founder member of Bazooka Joe

Dan Barson, Mike's brother, was the singer in Bazooka Joe, a north London rock and roll revival outfit that had started out in 1970, led at that time by John Ellis. He left in 1974 to form The Vibrators and went on to play with The Stranglers and Peter Hammill among others, a great example of the kind of musician who embraced punk and New Wave, having roots in pub-rock. Dan was with the band in the mid-1970s, and brother Mike used to go to see them with his mates. "Bazooka Joe was *the* local rock & roll band.

We used to see them a lot," says Chris. "Once they'd seen the Sex Pistols they had a bit of an epiphany and changed." In the post-punk world Bazooka Joe is better known as being Stuart Goddard's first band. Goddard became Adam Ant, a charming example of life imitating art, as there's a lyric in "Rockin' in Ab" that goes, "I'll have a cup of tea and then I'll change me name"— and it's a lyric that isn't lost on Suggs, either.

I'd always thought that this was a Madness song, because it sounds as if it could have been written by any number of them. Suggs' voice is distinctive and very comfortable with the lyric, although he admits to "having my 'Buddy Holly' voice on at one point in the song." The title, which, predictably enough, doesn't feature in the song, is a nod to the music hall question, "What do you get if you throw a piano down a pit-shaft?" Answer: A flat miner—Boom! Boom!! Also, predictably, it's not in Ab at all, but C. I'm not sure that there's an Ab in the entire song. Not an intentional one, anyway. As a self-taught saxophonist, Lee always thinks in flats rather than in sharps—even if a tune has what the rest of the world would think of as one sharp in the key signature, Thommo will think of it as a flat. It doesn't seem to have held him back.

"Rockin' in Ab" kicks off with a drum introduction, then rolls around the main riff a couple of times—"it's lifted from 'Beatnik Flyer' by Johnny and the Hurricanes," Chris confides, "and Bazooka Joe used to cover that, too." Then we're into the vocal with the occasional Buddy Holly hiccup. Twice around the verse, up to the middle eight, then:

Instrument!

Just about the only proper guitar solo on the whole album is heralded by this fabulous introduction. Perhaps they hadn't decided on who would take a solo here and just shouted "Instrument!" on the guide, but it's very endearing. It reminds me of one of the finest moments in Dr Feelgood's recording career. In "Down at The Doctor's" there's a harmonica solo, followed by a guitar solo, then Lee Brilleaux announces "Eight bars of piano," and the band solemnly chugs away for eight bars. There isn't a single, solitary note of piano to be heard in the entire tune. Genius.

CJ Foreman never had any intention of picking up the guitar initially. "I took up the guitar in 1976 when I got a tax rebate and Lee suggested I buy one," says Chris. "I got a Waltone semi-acoustic and started mucking around with it round at Mike's house, but I really wasn't that interested." It seems that there's a link between employment and guitarists—Chuck Berry reckoned he only pursued his musical career once it started paying more than his painting job. Chris again—"When I got the sack as a painter and decorator I started to play the guitar by listening to Dr Feelgood." The original line-up of the Feelgoods from Canvey Island in Essex was an inspiration to a lot of pre-punk bands, and was a refreshing change from the predominant prog-rock at the time. Singer Lee Brilleaux even gave Dave Robinson five hundred quid to finance the first release on Stiff Records. Guitarist Wilko Johnson—who, incidentally, had left by the time they recorded "Down at The Doctor's"— wrote some great songs, had that machine-gun style of playing his guitar and was a sight to behold. It's no surprise that he slotted in really well with Ian Dury's Blockheads for a spell in the early 1980s. Wilko and Chris have something in common, too—they're both left-handed, yet play right-handed guitar. Marc Ribot, ex-Lounge Lizard and stalwart of Tom Waits' band, is also a Southpaw who plays guitar right-handed. I had thought that Kev, Chris's substitute when Foreman 'retired' for a couple of years during 'that difficult Dangermen period,' was carefully selected for similar sinister reasons, but it turns out that it missed a generation—Kev plays regular right-handed guitar and his son is a left-hander who plays right-handed.

When talking about his contribution to *One Step Beyond*, Chris says "there's a lot going on on these tracks—Mike doubled loads of keyboards, but on this album we just left my guide guitars on." The guitar parts, like guide vocals, would often be replaced or at least double-tracked, but time was pressing here, and it seems likely that once Chris's guitar sound was set they left it at that for a lot of the songs. Well, not quite, according to Chris. Both Wilko Johnson and Lynval Golding from The Specials recommended H & H amps, so Foreman bought one for the recording session. Alan Winstanley wasn't too impressed, so he and Clive hired a Fender Twin valve amp for the guitar. Chris swears that on a couple of occasions he moved the microphone from the Fender to his own amp and the production team didn't even spot it. "Nah! I don't believe that!" exclaims Alan. "The guitar is so secondary to the piano and sax that Alan didn't notice," Foreman insists.

When asked about early influences, Chris lists the usual suspects of Prince Buster and Ian Dury, but also Alex Harvey and Roxy Music, which may not be obvious when first listening to *One Step Beyond*, but Chris says that a lot of musical influences are sub-conscious. He adds that Ronnie Lane's songs from *Ooh La La* were important to him, too, and it's interesting that it's The Faces' songs he singles out rather than just Ronnie Wood's guitar playing. It's well documented that Sex Pistol Glen Matlock was a big Faces fan, and he chose to play the Lane song "Debris" at the Ian Dury tribute night at London's Brixton Academy (of Jack-The-Lademy) in 2000 with guests Lee Thompson, his hero (and mine) Davey Payne, Mick Jones from The Clash, drummer Chris Musto with yours truly way down the list on piano. Fitting that Madness wrapped up the pre-Blockheads part of that evening with a Kilburns song and a few favourites of their own following Matlock's set.

During my conversation with Chris round at his place about *One Step Beyond* he'd dig out various records to give me examples of what they were listening to at the time, then go off at a tangent—just like I did in the previous paragraphs!—and play more recent purchases (he'd just got an Ernest Ranglin album that delighted him), so what comes across is his ongoing love for music and willingness to share it. The man's an evangelist.

*　*　*

After the guitar/instrument solo, the "Beatnik Flyer" riff rolls around a couple of times before the last two verses, outro and rock and roll ending wraps everything up in a cosy two-and-a-half minutes. Clive Langer's comment on the song was that Madness were "tipping their hat to their rock & roll influences,

'See You Later, Alligator' and all that sort of thing—rock and roll being really close to ska anyway. Anti-hippie music." Suggs reckons that in the early days "Rockin' in A*b*" went down really well with "even the most hardened ska fans," though he recounts one unsavoury incident when Dan Barson sang "Jailhouse Rock" with the band. "All the Bazooka Joe teddy-boy fans were there and our skinhead fans were there and it kicked off a bit." This must have been early days, possibly before The Invaders became Madness, because John Hasler was still drumming. "Someone threw a Party Seven which hit John and knocked him out," says Suggs. A Party Seven was the equivalent of a six-pack, but in one giant tin for you to take home for after hours drinking. A masterpiece of marketing, a Party Seven didn't even contain seven pints! Just for the record, the third Madness album *wasn't* named after it.

The attitude in the band regarding "Rockin' in A*b*" shows up the differences in age between them. Once everyone's the wrong side of forty, three or four years isn't important, but the difference between seventeen and twenty-one is immense. Suggs, Mark and Woody never saw Bazooka Joe while Lee, Chris and Mike were pretty seasoned fans. "I'd never heard of Bazooka Joe," says Woody, "and to me it was just a throwaway rock and roll track. Very pub-rock." Mark thinks that

Mike must have been taught the song by his brother, or maybe had a live tape of it as Bazooka Joe never recorded or released it. His also remembered that comedienne Arabella Weir was one of the backing singers in Bazooka Joe at one point, the delightfully named 'Lil-lettes.'

Although Suggs and Clive romantically remember the ska fans liking this rock and roll song and "anti-hippie music" united certain outsider factions, Mike remembers Bazooka Joe doing a reggae version of "Why Do Fools Fall in Love?" and that their teddy-boy following didn't get it at all. "Some people are so stupid," he says before observing that there is a large faction of redneck rockabilly fans who are right-wing, but love black music, and they mirror the right-wing skinheads who similarly love black music. I don't think that this is the bond that Langer has in mind…

"Rockin' in Ab" is a very lairy sounding track, though. Because it's sung in London English, rather than the Transatlantic drawl that so many rock and roll revivalists adopt, it has a 'nutty' flavour to it. The use of a great, booming reverb on the snare drum at well-selected moments puts you in mind of dub rather than rock and roll, but the sound is held together by the guitar style, both the rhythm parts and the solo. The back-beat ska skank isn't anywhere to be heard and, for once, the saxophone is part of the rhythm section, playing a complimentary riff to the "Beatnik Flyer" section from after the solo to the end. The tambourine in the last verse is a typical Clive Langer touch to pick the song up: playing the song at that speed probably meant that it was out of the question to kick the last verse up a key. Too many notes.

Not much saxophone, so not much in the way of observation from Lee except that "Mike suggested covering it—and the rest is history." Then, after a bit of a pause: "Great lyric." It's very much a lyric-led song, in fact, unlike many of the originals on *One Step Beyond*, and the instrumental section is very short. Quite traditional, in fact. "Great song, great lyric which really suited us," says Suggs, making reference to rehearsing in the church hall, cups of tea and all those images that infiltrate English pop songs, in spite of more American musical styles and structures. And calling your girlfriend your 'bird' dates it perfectly, bringing to mind British sitcoms like "Rising Damp," "The Likely Lads" and, of course, "The Liver Birds." It was set in the past even then, though, with references to pre-decimal money, 'three bob' being fifteen new pence. A nostalgic song, then, but you know what they say—nostalgia's not what it used to be.

Chapter 13—Mummy's Boy

I'm sure Mark could write more songs if he put his mind to it

—Mike Barson

Mark wrote this, didn't he? Good on 'im

—Woody

Mark Bedford should write more songs. He writes good songs

—Suggs

It seems, then, that the band is unanimous in its praise of Bedders' songwriting talents. Maybe the secret is to space them out. Less is more. "It's not one of your normal pattern of songs," says Lee. "Nice—my sort of lyric as well, a bit quirky—not your usual lovey-dovey song." Well, no, a song about a forty-year-old man living with his Mum who "makes

TERRY EDWARDS

sure his face ain't dirty" and holds his hand on the way to the pub of an evening can't really be described as 'lovey-dovey'!

Mark explains that "Mummy's Boy" was written while he was still at school. "It was a chance remark by one of my teachers who told me that he still lived at home with his parents. That set me thinking—in fact I found it quite shocking. Why would he still want to live at home? Because at that time I was a hot-headed teenager and independent. I wanted my own place." That chance remark led to the character being developed into the sort of outsider that Suggs is fascinated by, not a wilful eccentric, but someone who lives in their own world, harmless enough, but oblivious to the norm. "There seemed to be more of them (i.e. muttering oddballs) around when I was a kid," says Suggs. But then Soho does tend to attract people who march to the beat of a different drummer.

"Musically the song is close to Lee's description of 'The Nutty Sound'—part fairground, part music hall. I wanted it to sound like a theme tune for a comedy sitcom," Bedders continues. In fact it's reminiscent of the British sitcom "Steptoe & Son," both musically and in subject matter. In the programme Steptoe senior is the widower who is too old to go out on the rounds as a scrap dealer, and his able-bodied

· 134 ·

son wants to get away to make a life for himself, but is shackled by both his loyalty to his father and his fear of the outside world, were he to escape. The theme tune, written by Ron Grainer (who penned a lot of music for television, including the themes for "Doctor Who" and "Maigret") managed to conjure up the sights, sounds and almost the smells of the Steptoe yard, including the stables. The show, though irrefutably British, was successful in the US, rewritten as "Sanford & Son,", this time complete with a signature tune by Quincy Jones. It seems that this particular odd-couple really struck a chord. "With Madness that element of the tragic and the comic was there right from the start. 'Steptoe and Son' is so sad—that they're just stuck together," says Mark. On gigs promoting *The Dangermen Sessions*, the tune "Taller Than You Are" often morphed into the "Steptoe" theme at the end, courtesy of the monkeys in the horn section.

*   *   *

It's unusual to have such a wealth of songwriting talent in one band. In the year 2000 Madness were presented with an Ivor Novello Award for Outstanding Song Collection, and in many respects they are a songwriting collective. Only Woody doesn't get an individual name-check on the writing credits on *One Step Beyond*, Mark Bedford being the last in line, just a couple of tracks from the end. There is more money to be made in bands as the songwriter than just as a player, and this often leads to animosity and acrimonious separations (euphemistically referred to as 'musical differences'). Some groups deal with this by splitting everything equally, other songwriters redress the balance by giving non-writers a better share of profits from sales. Most take the money and run. Madness have a system whereby the named songwriter takes 50 percent of the royalty while the other 50 percent is divided among all seven band members. "Our songwriting splits are like the National Health Service—the sign of a civilised society," quips Mark. Many a true word spoken in jest.

"There isn't really a hierarchy in this band," says group-leader Mike Barson. "There's a lot of egos, a lot of pushing and pulling, but if you share the publishing the way we did then you don't get the arguments," he continues. "And it's fair." Chris Stamp, co-manager of The Who with Kit Lambert from 1964 until the mid-1970s, explains in the sleeve notes to the CD reissue of *A Quick One* that he'd negotiated a publishing deal (for cash!) on behalf of Roger Daltrey, Keith Moon and John Entwistle, which explains the inclusion of their songs on that album.

This was quite a coup as Pete Townshend was obviously the songwriter that mattered in the band. They each got five hundred quid, which was a very pretty penny in those days, and an astute bit of management. I guess that's one way to keep everybody happy, but in the long run, the fifty–fifty system works admirably for Madness.

Ironically, while the songwriting royalties have been divided to everyone's satisfaction, with the main writer receiving the plaudits and the entire band of musicians reaping a fair income in proportion to their input, there is a dispute as to who came up with the idea in the first place! Dave Robinson tells me that he'd seen too many bands split up over royalties and suggested the fifty–fifty split. Woody recalls their lawyer for the Stiff contract, Paul Woolf, recommending that whatever the band agreed on at that time, that they should stick with it. John Hasler, who by that time had taken over as manager, said that he was aware that there were some "strong personalities in the band, and once they'd worked out that the money was in songwriting, then they would push to get their own songs on the album, so I came up with the fifty–fifty formula." He modified the idea with some input from his father.

"Mummy's Boy" really is a perfect example of the Madness songwriting collective. "This song is half an

idea," says Mark—well, that's his 50 percent then!—
"and there are lots of different musical parts within
the song which were added when we recorded it." Lee
says that it goes in three stages—"the rocky bit, the
poppy bit, the sad bit. Reminds me of 'The Last of the
Teenage Idols' by Alex Harvey." There were two parts
originally, "the up/happy bit, then the reflective bit,"
Mark explains. "The 'punk' ending wasn't there when
we first played it, it was added later—because the original idea is so short!" Refining and honing a song has a
lot to do with the arrangement, and there is a Pacific-
Ocean-sized grey area as to what is actually writing
and what is arrangement. The fifty–fifty deal brushed
that knotty problem aside. Bedders "unashamedly
acknowledges" that Mike Barson helped out a lot on
this song, and Mike says that there are "seven musicians and several songwriters in the band, and what
comes out at the end is something you couldn't envis-
age on your own."

   Barso wasn't sure about Mark in the early days. On
the one hand Bedders was really excited to be playing
stuff he'd never heard before—"I'd never played ska or
reggae before and came away from the first rehearsal,
having borrowed someone else's bass, with huge blis-
ters on my hands!"—and from Mike's perspective
here was a somewhat green kid who hadn't heard half
of the stuff they were covering before. Speaking to

Mike during the recording sessions for *The Liberty of Norton Folgate* (2008), it's clear that he was glad he'd not gone on first impressions. "There are some great musicians in the band, especially Bedders," he says. "I used to think that there was nothing to bass playing, but when we tried a couple of demos without him it just didn't work out, it wasn't swinging. Mark came in and it was just effortless—he got it straight away." I had the same experience the previous year when Mark kindly came in and helped out on a session that I produced for Department S when they covered Alvin Stardust's glam hit "My Coo Ca Choo." The chords aren't exactly challenging, but he really made it swing. Hats off.

*   *   *

"Mummy's Boy" kicks off with what could be a 'sting' from a TV sitcom—Chris thought it might be copied from Leonard Rossiter's "Rising Damp," but that, funnily enough, is more of a pastiche of the film *The Sting*, Scott Joplin being in vogue when that was first broadcast—and we're straight into two verses followed by a middle eight. It's a middle seven-and-a-half, actually, as there's a characteristically quirky half-bar at the end of it. The first two verses are repeated, followed again by the middle eight, which, this time, is a middle-eight-and-a-bit as the last bar of it is five beats this time—those Madness boys do like to keep you on your toes—then there is the drop down, semi-reggae interlude.

Written in a more innocent time, where we'd snigger behind our hands at the mummy's boy, who is a bit of a harmless simpleton, the lyrics make us all a little uncomfortable these days. The song's author is well aware of it—"On reflection, the line '…she was twelve and he was thirty,' was a mistake because it sent the song in a different direction. Today it also takes on a much darker meaning…I think it's best to listen to it as it was written—as a teenager who wondered if the adult world was going to be how he imagined it." To me, that recent reappraisal certainly makes a lot of sense.

After the interlude the band kicks off into what Chris calls "the token punk bit with Suggs doing a Les Dawson bit at the end." Suggs says that he didn't realise until quite recently that he'd stuck in the 'knickers, knackers, knockers' bit, which he calls "the Benny Hill pervert thing" at the end. It's reminiscent of both "Yakety Sax" by Boots Randolph, best known as the outro music to many a Benny Hill Show, and Ian Dury & the Blockheads' "Blackmail Man," which closes *New Boots and Panties* (the album title refers to the items of clothing that you should always buy new, all other garments being perfectly acceptable second-hand). Suggs echoes Bedders' sentiments these days, saying "I kind of turned him into a pervert at the end, which is a bit of a shame, really. I think I just got over excited!"

This song is a good example of a tune written by a bassist. The melody follows the bass-line for quite a lot of the time, something that also characterises songs written by Jem Moore of Serious Drinking and The Scapegoats. Serious Drinking modelled themselves somewhat on Madness, having two frontmen, guitar, bass, drums and keyboards, but no sax. The verse is almost all sing-a-long-a bass-line, the middle eight less so, but the vocal line in the interlude, despite being different rhythmically, just follows the root notes of the bass. Woody follows suit a bit here, too. "Nick, my guitar playing brother, used to say that I had this weird habit of playing 'tympani-like' on the drums," he says, "playing along with the melody. The drums go very well with the vocals." Orchestral kettle drums tend to be tuned to the main root notes, too, so that fits very nicely. Woody also manages to get a full-on roll round all his tom-toms at the end to introduce the punk section, and it must have been a relief for him to be let off the leash for once, and not just stick to a solid beat at the behest of Langer and Winstanley.

Let's leave the last word to Lee Thompson, who is bit of a fan of Mark Bedford the songwriter. "He should've carried on writing. If he wanted to, he could write a lyric or a tune. 'One Better Day' (the Top 20 single that Bedders wrote with Suggs, from the *Keep Moving* album) brings a tear to my eye. Fantastic."

14

According to the back sleeve of *One Step Beyond* there are seven songs on each side, and at the end of side two "Mummy's Boy" is swiftly followed by "Chipmunks Are Go!" Imagine the looks of glee on every young rude boy and rude girl's face when the intro to "Madness" comes blasting out of the speakers unannounced—a secret track! Must be a collectors' item!

Well, this particular collectors' item sold hundreds of thousands of copies. The cassette version included "Madness" but didn't list it, and in later years the CD version kept up the pretence. On the box set of the first six studio albums, *The Lot*, the conceit remained, though by now the publishing credits acknowledged its existence in very small print, referring to it as a "surprise track, not listed on the sleeve." Among the

band there is a hazy collective memory of not wanting the B-side of their first single on the album, even
if it was a re-recording. "We were having pangs of
guilt that 'The Prince' was on the album anyway, so
we didn't think that 'Madness' would be on it—then
we found it funny that we'd have the track the band
was named after on the album, but not even mention it," says Mark. Chris agrees, and Lee adds that
Madness "always tried to keep the B-sides off the
albums, try to keep it V.F.M.—Value For Money for
the punters."

Ian Dury and the Blockheads had three top ten hits
on Stiff, but Dury was adamant that they were not
on albums, either the A-side or the B-side. Robinson
must have lost quite a few album sales because of that
policy and he was in no mood to do the same with
Madness, but he evidently agreed with the band—or
at least let them have their way on this occasion—
and sequenced the album without the inclusion of
their self-named calling card. So how did it get on
the record? It was all down to Clive Langer. "The
artwork had been done before we decided to put
'Madness' on it. Robbo said that we couldn't put it
on because the artwork was finished, and I remember
saying, 'of course you can, just stick it on'—how brilliant for everyone who listens to it!" Mystery solved,
then—it's always been on the album, but never

credited. I guess the real collector's item would be the copy without "Madness" on it.

*   *   *

"Prince Buster's 'Madness' was one of the Blue Beat singles I bought at Berwick Street market," says Suggs, "and I particularly liked it as it was a 12-bar, but not quite, and it had a nice lyric which I thought would suit us as a band." When they first played "Madness" the band was called The Invaders. For one show they even changed their name to Morris & the Minors as another 'Invaders' had sprung up. It's well documented that Chris said they should call themselves after a song in their set, then groaned when "Madness" was selected—he must have wanted them to be "The Bed and Breakfast Men" or something…Anyway, "Madness" was one of many ska covers they did at the time— Mike recalls "Feeling So Fine" by The Gladiators and a ska version of Stevie Wonder's "For Once in My Life" being learned around the same time.

Perhaps Chris's disappointment at "Madness" being chosen is down to him thinking that their reading of it was nothing special—"Now, 'One Step Beyond,' we really did something with that, made it distinct," he says. "I don't think this track is—it's a straighter cover." Lee's also a bit down on his own performance, too. "I really wanted to do a big old growling solo on this," he says—'growling' being a technique whereby you shout or sing while playing the sax, making the reed really vibrate exaggeratedly (check out R&B legend Earl Bostic to hear this sound in all its glory). "I wasn't confident enough to do it, what with the tuning problems," Lee continues, "so I was a bit disappointed with the solo on the album. The Two Tone version was a throwaway, anyway." The sax solo on the album is drenched in Langer and Winstanley's harmoniser effect, too. They were amused when I told them that when I went into the studio with The Higsons for the first time (Spaceward in Cambridgeshire, 1981) they plugged in an Eventide harmoniser almost before I got my sax out of the case—Clive and Alan had unwittingly invented the sax sound that every studio technician aspired to in the early 1980s.

I suppose it is a pretty straight cover of the song, but what else could you do with it? No point being intellectual about it, it's just a great party song—"Fuck Art, Let's Dance" as the t-shirt says. I like the three false endings that close the tune. If you clap along from the beginning (go on, everyone else in the studio does) you realise that the second false ending has you clapping on the beat, rather than the off-beat. That's because the false endings are all seven beat bars (four + three, if you like). Now I'm not pretending that there's any great plan here, it just sounds good and quirky, but it's fitting that 'Madness,' the word, has seven letters, "Madness" the tune has some bars with seven beats in it and Madness the band has seven members. Seven— lucky for some, but not Dr Feelgood. Wilko Johnson said he'd walk if "Lucky Seven" was included on the album *Sneakin' Suspicion*. It was. He did.

Suggs enthusiastically took his copy of Prince Buster's "Madness" into the punk shop, "Boy," in King's Road, Chelsea, to play it to someone he knew worked there, saying "this is the sort of music my band's going to do." He was met with complete bemusement and ridicule— "trumpets and everything? You're joking, you're never going to get anywhere," was the considered opinion in punk rock days. Brass instruments were lost in action, along with Glenn Miller. Some thirty years later and of course Madness play it at every gig still, with Suggs spelling the name out over the introductory drum beat. After all these years you'd think he'd know it backwards, but I've heard him dyslexically kick it off with M-A-D-E-E-S-S! It's easy to find yourself over-refreshed towards the end of the evening, though.

*   *   *

We thought it was ripping off the fans to release loads of singles, so we always made sure that the B-sides were new songs or totally different versions
— 'Reasonable' Chris Foreman

I know that this book is about the album *One Step Beyond*, but it seems fitting here to include a few words about the B-sides of the singles that are included on the album. Madness spent more weeks on the UK singles charts than any other artist during the 1980s (no mean feat considering they didn't even release anything for the last three years of that decade), so the singles are as important as the albums and some of the B-sides here could easily have wound up on *One Step Beyond* had the dice fallen differently...

B-Sides

Mistakes (B-side of "One Step Beyond")

> *They were playing a two chord vamp, and I just went into the next room and wrote the lyrics.*
> —John Hasler

In many respects this is the most important song in the collection. It's a very early song, but it resonates with much of the following Madness catalogue. "The subject matter was what you came to expect from Madness in later years," says Bedders, and you can certainly draw a line directly from "Mistakes" to "One Better Day," "Yesterday's Men" and "Norton Folgate." Cathal says that "Mistakes" has his favourite lyric with "such an astute observation of life at a young age. It's way ahead of its time. And poignant. I'm a massive fan of the darker aspect of Madness."

Lee thinks it should have been an album track, and it's a big favourite of Alan Winstanley's, too, but it would have stuck out a bit, despite the subject matter of some of the songs that did make the cut. The feel of this track is darker, too. Musically it's modelled on Elvis Costello's "Watching the Detectives," what with the organ sounds and Chris's trademark twangy guitar sound. The outro is the precursor to the wonderful outros the band plays live on "Grey Day" some twenty-five–thirty years later, too. Perhaps the "One Step Beyond" single is the perfect Madness artefact— the A-side's a dance-floor filler, and the B-side looks through the bottom of an emptying glass, darkly. From womb to grave, as the lyric says.

Nutty Theme (Additional Track on "One Step Beyond" 12" Single)

This was an attempt to create our own genre.
—Chris Foreman

"We didn't want to be 'ska' or 'Two Tone,' but to have our own sound," says Suggs. Both he and Chris say that the "Steptoe & Son" theme was at the front of their minds here, too, along with "Billy Bentley," a

Kilburn & the High Roads song. "Hello, good evening and welcome," the catchphrase of TV personality David Frost, opens the song, mirroring Dury's "Hello Playmates," which has music hall comedian Arthur Askey's catchphrase at the top of "Billy Bentley." Suggs continues the Dury references with "been down the High Road," and yet another smattering of everyone's favourite percussion instrument, the skulls, before shouting:

Rhythm!!

Mark says that "Nutty Theme" was intended as an opening track, so this would be an introduction to the band, of sorts. Woody and Bedders, the rhythm section, although among the younger element of the band, were really solid. Clive liked them for more practical, even selfish reasons. "Mark and Woody were really great to work with—because they didn't interfere with the finished product!" he says. Musically, Woody came from a predominantly rock and jazz/fusion background. While playing the standards "All Right Now," "House of the Rising Sun" and the like in school bands, as we all did, he was deeply into John McLaughlin, Steve Hillage, Santana and Herbie Hancock. The only reggae artist he was aware of was Bob Marley. Mark's early bands also played blues, rhythm and blues and "vaguely contemporary American stuff" (he says, suitably vaguely), but he was listening to a lot of Motown at the time, too.

"When I first joined the band," says Woody, "all they ever went on about was Kilburn & the High Roads. I'd never seen them—or even heard of them." Woody was happy playing his 'hippie' music on his Ajax drum kit (made by Eddy Ryan, drum-maker to the stars including Led Zeppelin's John Bonham and Ric Parnell, son of bandleader Jack. Ric played Mick Shrimpton, drummer in Spinal Tap—now there's a claim to fame), but he knew the time had come to lose a few tom-toms and trade his bright yellow kit for something more fitting when Madness started getting it together.

*   *   *

The song's straight back in with two more verses over the twelve bar structure, then Suggs introduces:

Melody!!

And so the familiar chromatic run-down on the piano in triplets (that's three notes to a beat), where a drum roll might be, and we are in the realm of Mike Barson. Clive Langer has great admiration for Mike's melodies, and it's interesting to discover what he was listening to and learning on the piano as a nipper, which took him in the direction of songs such as "My Girl" and "Bed and Breakfast Man." Records would filter down from his brother Dan and his mate, Paul, into Mike's pool of influences. There are quite a few piano-based singer–songwriters in the list. "I used to listen to Elton John's *Tumbleweed Connection*, and I liked Carole King and Joni Mitchell," he says, qualifying it with, "let's get the naff ones out the way before I mention the good ones! Some of the records I listened to, the piano-playing does sort of affect you. 'Fire in the Hole' by Steely Dan had a really nice piano solo on it which I listened to again and again, although I never attempted to play it." Mike pauses before saying, "Steely Dan's a bit complicated." Yes, quite.

Tamla Motown and The Kinks get mentioned, the latter more for Ray Davies' piano-led songs rather than the guitar-based ones, and Cat Stevens' *Tea for the Tillerman* is on Barso's list, too, "Sad Lisa" being a tune that he spent hours learning at his brother's in Crouch End. When Stevens converted to Islam and turned his back on making music, he sold his instruments, several of which came up for sale at a rehearsal studio that Madness frequently used. Bedders is still the proud owner of a Guild acoustic guitar that once belonged to Cat Stevens, "and it sounds even better with age," he says.

Obviously Mike learned a lot of old ska and reggae tunes, but he says that it's very hard to hear exactly what's going on on them—"you can't hear what the organ player's doing because of the mix. There's a bit of guesswork involved." He also resorted to playing 45s at 33 1/3 to slow them down enough to catch the sequence of notes, "but obviously it made it a different key when you put it back to 45, so it was pretty difficult. I used to buy songbooks, I definitely had a Motown book with all the chords in it, but I was such a lazy bum that I never learnt how to read music, so it took ages." Dave Brubeck's "Take Five" (actually written by his saxophonist, Paul Desmond) was another that the Barson brothers all worked out, and Mike's proud of sorting out the middle section by himself—no mean feat—but he never really went down the jazz route. "My older brother was into modern jazz. He had a five-album box set by Keith Jarrett which, as far as I could hear, had one good song on it!" Bedders is the only member of Madness who's pursued the jazz connection (with BUtterfield 8), but Chris has his moments in the odd guitar solo in concert, not exactly jazz, but just to the left of pop—rather like the piano solo on Nick Lowe's "Breaking Glass," in fact.

*   *   *

"Nutty Theme" closes with a final verse, and once round the twelve-bar sequence for Thommo to do his very finest Davey Payne impression a la "Common as Muck" (the B-side of "Reasons to Be Cheerful"), which was definitely a nod back to the Kilburns rather than the Blockheads. It's a perfect B-side rather than an album track, and although it was an attempt to create their own genre outside of the new wave of ska, without too much hindsight it's obviously in the shadow of the old-guard of jovial East End pub-rock. Nothing wrong with that. By the way, it's nominally penned by Suggs and Lee, but Mark reckons that "Lee hummed the tune, Suggs chipped in with the lyrics and Mike would have fleshed the chords out," another example of the fifty–fifty splits levelling the playing field.

Stepping Into Line (B-side of "My Girl")

> *A joy to play live.*
> —Lee Thompson

The Business, the self-proclaimed 'definitive singles collection' that has all these B-sides on disc one of a set of three, erroneously credits "Stepping Into Line" to Suggs and Bedders. It's actually another tune from the pen of Mr Hasler. "John wrote the first half of the words and I wrote the other half," says Suggs. Chris describes it as "my moment of glory, trying to keep it all together!" Well, it does race away with itself quite a bit, but that's youthful enthusiasm for you. And they manage to sneak in a crafty little key change right at the end of the song, too. Suggs reckons it's in the same vein as "Nutty Theme" in that "Stepping Into Line" veers away from Two Tone, but it's very heavy on the off-beat guitar, so they didn't stray too far from the reservation on this one.

In The Rain (B-side of "My Girl" 12" Single)

> *I don't know about you, but I'm a sucker for weather. My feeling is that if you put weather in a song, there's very little else you need to do.*
> —Tom Waits introducing "November" in concert in
> Hammersmith, London, 2004

This is probably the most Two Tone sounding tune Madness ever did. The organ sounds are straight out of the Jerry Dammers manual and Woody's even got the snare drum tuned way up to timbale altitude for those Sugar Minott-style rim-shot fills. The vocal is quite deadpan, delivering a tale of being stood up. Suggs agrees that the organ sound is really good and adds that "the drums were more metallic." Mark tells me that this was recorded in London's Basing Street Studios shortly after the band had taken their first trip to America and Chrissy Boy remembers Suggs having a cold when this was recorded—"and you can hear it."

I thought he was just doing a Terry Hall impression, but maybe he'd caught the 'flu doing all that standing in the rain. Sounds to me like there's a chorus in this song—maybe the songwriting style is about to change…

Deceives the Eye (On the "Work, Rest & Play" EP)

I was in with a bad crowd. Barso & Thommo.
—Chris Foreman

The three tunes that accompanied "Night Boat to Cairo" on the "Work, Rest & Play" EP were also recorded on a BBC session for Mike Read in January 1980 (alongside "My Girl," which had been released just before Christmas). "Deceives the Eye" told the true tale of Chris Foreman being out and about with Thommo and Mike in Luton and finding himself on the wrong side of the law. "A few of us enjoyed the pleasures of shoplifting," Chris explains. "I got caught, my Dad went to court with me. He blamed himself, but it wasn't his fault." It's an amusing, chirpy little song—victimless crime and all that malarkey—and yet again it's a song that nods its head to Ian Dury. "Razzle in My Pocket" the B-side of "Sex & Drugs & Rock & Roll," tells the tale of Dury being caught shoplifting in the shopping arcade in South Street, Romford. I dearly love this tune because there, on record, was a real place that I went to every Saturday after my piano lesson—The Quadrant Arcade, Romford, was immortalised in song and it brought a great big smile to my face. I was a civilian, though. Never had the bottle to nick anything.

This new breed of song is certainly more accomplished than the earlier B-sides. The music is largely written by Bedders, and the melody is very bass-led. It's not quite as much of a sing-a-long-a bassline as "Mummy's Boy," but you can hear where it's coming from and it suits the narrative admirably. Interesting to note that the title only appears at the end—okay, it appears twice at the end, and it's not an A-side, but it's in very select company along with "The Prince."

The Young and the Old (On the "Work, Rest & Play" EP)

> *This was about getting drunk in the pub and noticing how old people acted younger as the evening went on.*
>
> —Suggs

And a very astute observation it is, for a man of such tender years! There are some great lyrics here such as "age creeping backwards as it gets late" and "wisdom comes up later and goes down the pan," graphically chronicling 'a good night out.' I wonder if the bizarre Drink-Aware and 'Please Drink Responsibly' campaigns are Madness-Aware? I can feel an advertising campaign coming on…Thommo, a huge fan of Suggs as wordsmith says, "another great Suggs lyric. He's streets ahead, and on *The Liberty of Norton Folgate* he's really upped the ante." The song's co-written by Mike Barson and it's organ-led until the fast handclaps come in and send it careering on its way. A taste of things to come.

Don't Quote Me on That (On the "Work, Rest & Play" EP)

> *"Mistakes", "Nutty Theme" and "Stepping Into Line" were all contenders for the album. "In The Rain" and the "Work, Rest & Play" EP were newer songs, the bridge between* One Step Beyond *and* Absolutely
>
> —Woody

"The riff is lifted from 'Bush Doctor' by The Music Doctors," says Chris, and fires up his Wurlitzer jukebox to play me the original. Peter Tosh had a hit with a song by the same name, and Tosh's publishers thought that some money was on the cards as a Madness co-write. Chris gleefully whips the single out of the jukebox and shows me who wrote the Music

Doctors' tune. It says 'Thompson' on the label. Nice grey area for the writing credit, then.

Lyrically the song came about when one of the music papers printed an interview with Cathal that intimated he was a racist. "Lots of stupid stuff was said about us and racism," says Suggs, "when we were on the road with black people, friends of ours, of Cathal in particular—and he was the one getting castigated." John Hasler told me the amusing tale of Eddie Josephs, a black guy that Madness auditioned to play drums in the early days. After the audition he said, "you guys play too much reggae—I don't want to join the band!"

"I was aggrieved by the interview, that my comments were misconstrued. I dunno—I wasn't all that eloquent then," Cathal explains retrospectively. "I was all tongue-tied. 'Don't Quote Me' was a groove. Until I really started songwriting I'd just free-form over a groove, one take, that was it. I remember the energy of delivering that track and trying to be clever in an obtuse way, but I don't know if I succeeded at all, really...I've accepted who I was then, and see it as a completely honest time-capsule of that kid. And I find it really refreshing." Suggs remembers Lee coming up with hook, "It's all eggs, bacon, beans and a fried slice," so there was more to it than just free-forming, but it's got a great, immediate feel.

The sound is nice and homogenous between the three EP tracks, all done in one session with Clive and Alan at the controls. Woody came up with the title "Work, Rest & Play"—"I don't know how it came about, I just remember suggesting the title," he says—and it starts with a Night Boat to Cairo and ends up in Maggie's Caff in Liverpool Road, London N1. There was a block in Liverpool Road that housed Madness's offices, Two Tone's office and Station Agency, the booking agents who looked after Madness and many other bands including The Higsons. The drummer from The Jam had a studio there for a while, too, but it's now gone the way of all real estate in London nowadays—expensive and residential.

*   *   *

There go the B-sides, then, and I make no apologies for including them in a book about the album, because in these days of album retrospectives and reissues, you'll always find such recordings tacked onto the end of a CD—well, there's space for them now, whereas you couldn't get more than forty minutes on an album. But then maybe that was a good thing.

Chapter 15—
Chipmunks Are Go!

My father used to sing that Marines chant because he'd been in the American corps of military engineers.

—Cathal

It's strange that of all the tracks on the album, this little throwaway piece of under a minute divides opinion more than any other. All cards on the table, I never liked "Chipmunks Are Go," never understood why it was on the record and thought it was a bit too self-knowing, trying a bit too hard. I couldn't work out where this bit of American militaristic bravado— performed largely with a North London accent— fitted into the British new wave of ska via punk and pub rock. Having the 'all-boys-together' chant close the record sounded like a forced bit of merriment to me, like New Year's Eve when the world and his wife insists on drinking to excess to prove that they know how to have a good time.

There are several viewpoints in the band, too. Mark sees it as a nod to the culture of Americana prevalent at the time, which links it to "Believe Me" and the like, plus the 1950s fashions that shops like Flip in Covent Garden were making a pretty penny from. "Members of the band were wearing 50s suits, or maybe 60s mohair suits but with brothel creepers, you know, not 'Jam' shoes," says Mark. Mike adds that "Cathal used to wear American airman's sunglasses, which I used to hate. I was more into British-style jackets, stuff like that. But we'd end the set with 'Chipmunks' and it went down well, but it didn't make me think 'Wow, we've got to do another piece like that for the next album!'"

"We did it as an encore, all at the front of the stage," says Mark, and it's this that sends shivers down his rhythm pal's spine. "I had absolutely no love for this whatsoever," says Woody. "It became part of the set after the album was out and we had to go to the front of the stage at the end of the set, which was not my idea of fun—I like to be behind a drum-kit, 'please leave me alone, I don't want to do this silly chant!' And I've no idea why we did it. Absolutely no idea." John Hasler remains bemused by its inclusion, too—"should never have been on the album," he says. Chris recalls that they "just got a bit drunk and recorded it," while all Alan has to say is that "Chipmunks" was recorded in Eden Studios, whereas all the other vocals were done elsewhere. I think that's a diplomatic "no comment."

Clive Langer has a more relaxed view. "It's a great end to the album, good for kids. Just a bit of fun as far as I was concerned." Though he continues, "It's a bit aggressive—their aggressive side." Suggs tells me "we'd all get on the tube and start singing songs from those old American army movies when they're on the march," and Cathal describes the uniform that he and his crew sported—"We used to wear Lonsdale tops, Levis and sneakers, have crop haircuts and call ourselves The Chipmunks." Lee remembers a scene with the marines chanting as they marched in *The Boys in Company C*, the film that inspired "Razor Blade Alley," adding that *One Step Beyond* was such a fun album to make—"it was great doing it, just that gang mentality." Clive also points out that getting "Chipmunks" on the album was "Cathal stamping his authority on the album, like a gang's calling card," but also notes that Cathal's position in the group was ambiguous as he "wasn't a member of the band as such."

*   *   *

"I always felt insecure in the band, never totally safe," says Cathal. So, the leader of the gang who wasn't in the gang—kind of Groucho Marx in reverse—where does Cathal Smyth/Chas Smash fit in? He was the bassist in the first incarnation of the band, playing covers including "The Girl From Ipanema," "I'm Walkin'," "Poison Ivy" and "Just My Imagination," then left for a spell, after which he returned as fan-turned-Master of Ceremonies at Lee Thompson's request. As Thommo was particularly interested in the visual side of things, perhaps he thought there was something to be gained from there being one more person onstage, keeping himself and the audience on their toes. John Hasler remarked that Madness was one of the first bands to have an MC/dancer, "vibing everyone up" as he puts it, and it certainly inspired bands such as The Mighty Mighty Bosstones and Serious Drinking (who boasted three frontmen at their earliest gigs; safety in numbers).

Cathal's background is interesting. He says, "I'm a child of pop—Sweet, T Rex, Gary Glitter, Mud and Bowie, and I collected the weekly magazine *Word* which published the lyrics of songs in the Top Twenty [not to be confused Mark Ellen and David Hepworth's 21st Century publication of the same name]. At the same time I was listening to Savoy Brown (late 60s British blues band), Mahavishnu Orchestra and Gong. My Dad travelled a lot and brought records back from Europe. My uncles would play Dvorak, traditional Irish music, 'cod' Irish music, even 'Switched On Bach,' the first popular synthesiser album." So, what with some early stints living in Iran and Iraq, introducing him to Arabic music and culture, which the rest of us back home in Britain were oblivious to, Cathal has a wealth of musical experiences to draw on—but, at the time of recording *One Step Beyond*, they lay dormant.

*   *   *

I have this theory about classic albums—and I figure that if you've got this far in the book, you'll indulge me—and that is that they all have a weakness. For instance, with David Bowie's *Ziggy Stardust* it's the strange cover version, "It Ain't Easy" (apparently recorded two months before the main sessions and vying for a place with B-sides, so no wonder it sticks out a bit). I think it's the juxtaposition of classics next to a lesser track that makes an album loveable, believable or even 'human.' For me the best Beatles record is the White Album (and some tracks on that make me positively cringe—but not as much as practically the entire *Sgt Pepper's* record), but there is something in the ugly/beauty of it. The Japanese call it 'wabi-sabi,' meaning perfection in imperfection, and while I don't think it's wise to go into Eastern philosophy here— Monsieur Barso wasn't to become a Buddhist for some

years yet—I'd like to think that "Chipmunks Are Go"
is the track that makes the rest of the LP even more
loveable, believable and human. You know, on reflection, if "Madness" had been the last listed track on
One Step Beyond and "Chipmunks Are Go" was the
uncredited bonus track, the sense of balance would be
restored and I think I'd be more amenable to it.

And would you believe it? The title appears just
once, right at the end of the song. I don't know, you
wait for ages for a bus, then three come along all at
once...

Chapter 16—
A Porky Prime Cut

In the good old days of vinyl, a tradition sprang up of writing messages in the run-out grooves of the record. This was often alongside the cutting engineer's initials or nickname. Side one of *One Step Beyond*, the album, has "That Nutty Sound" scratched into it, and side two says, "Direct from Camden Town." The engineer was Steve (or SA).

However, the most famous of these monikers is "A Porky Prime Cut," the signature of George Peckham who started the practice. His mark can be found in the run-out grooves of the "One Step Beyond" seven inch ('Watch this—A Porky Prime Cut'). Countless thousands of pieces of vinyl of all shapes and sizes have the Porky scratchings, but this is how it came about: George started cutting records in the 1960s.

As a Liverpudlian he knew The Beatles and worked for them. He cut George Harrison's triple album *All Things Must Pass* in the UK and was flown out to America to do the same for the release there. This put the record manufacturer's nose out of joint and the engineer there insisted that the sound was wrong for the US and needed different EQ settings. Harrison wanted Porky's sound, and the disagreement continued. Porky cut the record and made a mark in the run-out groove next to the catalogue number. When the test-pressings returned from the factory they did not have mark on them, so Porky knew that they had gone against his client's wishes and cut the record elsewhere. Cue considerable egg on face! Harrison insisted that the record would not be released in that state, and that Porky recut the album. Peckham continued to sign his 'cuts' right up until he retired in around 2004. One of his longest personal messages was on Harrison's *Dark Horse* album in 1975—"Ooh George, you're such a Dark Horse—luv George/A Porky Prime Cut."

Epilogue

One Step Beyond is the product of a remarkable period of British music. Madness caught the second wind of the New Wave/Punk Rock explosion, close enough to it to be rooted in its predecessor, Pub Rock, but with the youth and vigour of the Do It Yourself ethos. Exciting, forward-looking times, but still bound by traditional studio technology and, in a way, traditional values. The band shot to fame just as Margaret Thatcher began to maul Britain, too. I still find it hard to believe that 2009 sees the thirtieth anniversary of the birth of Two Tone and the release of this debut album.

My main objective here, though, is not to make everyone feel old—including myself!—but to celebrate *One Step Beyond*. If this volume of 33 1/3 has made you discover or rediscover the album, play it again and inspire some conversation, then it's achieved what I wanted it to.

Resources

Books

Total Madness, by George Marshall, published by STP
The Two Tone Story, by George Marshall, published by STP
The Peel Sessions, by Ken Garner, published by BBC Books
Madness Songbook, published by Warner Brothers
Ian Dury Songbook, published by Blackhill Music
Guinness Book of British Hit Singles, by Gambaccini/Rice/Rice
Ian Dury & the Blockheads, Song by Song, by Jim Drury, published by Sanctuary

Film

Take it or Leave it—Madness/Stiff 1981. DVD release, Virgin 2002

Web

www.madness.co.uk
www.myspace.com/madnessofficial
www.myspace.com/mikebarson
www.mis-online.net

Also available in this series: